to **have** and to

Hold

You have and hold
the treasure of
Jesus!
Sharon Yoder

TO HAVE AND TO HOLD
Hope Restored for Single Women

Faith Builders Resource Group, 28500 Guys Mills Rd., Guys Mills, PA 16327

ISBN: 978-1-935972-07-5

Available from Christian Learning Resource. To order or request information, please call 1-877-222-4769 or email clr@fbep.org.

Faith Builders Resource Group is dedicated to building the Kingdom of God by partnering with conservative Anabaptist communities to identify needs and to address them with services and materials that honor Christ and strengthen His church. To learn more about Faith Builders Educational Programs, visit www.fbep.org.

Printed in the United States.

to *have* and to *Hold*

hope restored for **SINGLE WOMEN**

SHARON YODER

FAITH BUILDERS RESOURCE GROUP

CONTENTS

Acknowledgements   vii

Introduction   1

EXPLORING GOD'S PURPOSE

When Are You Going to Get Married?   7

Alone and a Single Rib   19

For This Cause   35

Why in the World Are There Singles?   55

ENVISIONING GOD'S PLAN

Shame Wears Fig Leaves   83

Embracing Femininity   103

Forsaken and Grieved   131

Enlarging Your Tent   155

EMBRACING GOD'S PATTERN

The Heart of Friendship   181

Lady-in-Waiting   197

The Heart at Home   219

Wearing the Glass Slippers   243

Endnotes   259

About Sharon   263

restoring hope

ACKNOWLEDGEMENTS

Unknown to me, the seed of this book dropped into my hands in the spring of 2003. Melvin Lehman, who taught "Singleness, Marriage & Family," invited me to speak on singleness. This happened in subsequent years which expanded my ideas on the subject.

In the spring of 2006, I was invited to speak at a women's banquet in Antrim, Ohio. The focus of the topic was bridging the gap between the single women and married women's world. Thanks, Antrim women, for the lovely banquet which gave birth to the idea of this book.

The next step was sharing the book idea with you, Steven and Cynthia. You envisioned the end product with total confidence. Steven, you were right—the class notes of "Singleness & Women" became the backbone for this book.

Certainly, I must include my deepest appreciation to the Resource Group which has made this whole endeavor a possibility. Credit for the organization and completion of the book project goes to you, Ernest. Matthew and Kyle, your contributions also are applauded.

Shari, you are an amazing woman. Your diplomacy, your knowledge, and your wisdom brought the book to a readable form. Thanks, Kristy Wadsworth, for your professional editing expertise. Grace, I admire your detailed editing skills, and your gracious gift of serving those who walk alone.

Thanks to Esther, Irene, Beatrice, Vivian, Anna, Yvonne, and Crista, my single friends, on staff at Faith Builders Educational Programs during this writing process. You are women of God whose prayers, encouragement, and love often gave wings to my spirit.

My thanks would not be complete without the acknowledgement of the 2000 mentoring group and other mentoring groups and friends from FBEP as well. You know who you are. Your gift of friendship has touched my life in significant ways; you also are on the pages of this book.

My humble thanks include Charlotta and Victor, Brandon and Marie, John and Barb, Merle and Amy, Melvin and Shelia, Evelyn and Lonnie, Gerald and Cathy, Stephe, Sharon, and Elaine. I extend my deepest appreciation to others who have been involved in some form or another in the book endeavor and are not named.

To my precious nieces and nephews—you have a special place in my heart. Thanks to my siblings and their spouses, Deb and Dave, Mark and Barb, Tim and Ruth, James and Gladys, Esther and Brent, for your love and support. I never feel single when I am with you! Mom and Dad, thanks for courageously embracing the path I have walked.

Finally, I owe all that has come from this book, to the glory of the Father and God of my Lord Jesus Christ. Without Him, this book would not be.

INTRODUCTION
Ere the Twain Shall Meet

Does life come in twos, or is it a single entity? Time revolves around the twins of day and night. A couple joins as husband and wife. Children count the animals that went into Noah's ark two by two. A farmer yokes his oxen. The chef prepares a candlelight dinner for a man and a woman. An electrician works with positives and negatives. A mathematician thinks in terms of addition and subtraction. When my aunt Emma thought in twos, she envisioned sugar and creamer sets. They were one of her life passions.

Aunt Emma collected many elegant, lovely, dainty, different, and sometimes odd-looking sugar and creamer sets. Several shelves in her china cabinet stored these sets. Sometimes she bought them new. Other times she found them by scrounging tables at garage sales. Whenever she discovered another unique sugar and creamer, she took the set home and made room for it on the shelf. Perhaps these sets symbolically completed something in my aunt Emma's life, as she never had—a husband. The sugars and creamers became the "china dolls" for the children she never had. They were her pride and joy as she told stories to those who had time to gaze upon them.

Eventually Aunt Emma moved into a smaller house, and she

could no longer store her many sets. As a token of love, Aunt Emma invited nieces and nephews to come to her home and pick out one set from her beloved collection. Although I was one of the last to arrive that day, she still had an ample amount of sets available to choose from.

My eyes roved over the pretty sets waiting in silence to be chosen. A single bone-colored creamer caught my attention, its delicate shape reminiscent of an oil lamp from millennia ago. Its tapered top and bottom edges, pencil-lined with gold, accentuated the slender handle with its delicate gold streak. The gentle curved spout was large enough for cream to flow generously. On the rounded sides of the creamer clung wisps of tiny blue and rose-colored wild flowers. "Aunt Emma," I asked, "where is its partner?"

She smiled and shook her head slightly. "I really don't know," she replied softly. "It is just a single one. If you pick that one, I have no sugar bowl to go with it," she added regretfully.

My gaze returned to the table, seeking one set that was meant for me. I found none. My eye kept admiring the beauty of the bone creamer with the wildflowers. I reached out to pick it up. The handle curved nicely between my right fingers as I cupped my left hand under its base. It fit. This creamer defines who I am. Alone, single—one who sits among twos. Perhaps one day I will stumble across its partner or its partner will find me.

* * * * * * *

I am a single woman. I have never married. Like the bone creamer, I am surrounded by a married world of pairs. I have not always done well accepting the gift of being single. At times

I have deeply longed for a husband and family. However, decades have passed, and I remain a single woman today.

Why do some people marry and others do not? Was this really the way it was meant to be? Could it perhaps have been God's original plan that all people marry? We seem to know instinctively that men and women were created not to walk alone, but in relationship with each other. Why then are there so many single people in the world?

My purpose in this book is to tangle with some of the questions I have just asked and explore God's intentions for single women. But I will speak to married women as well. The questions we ask and the answers we seek are not as different as you might think. Perhaps some of the ideas will introduce you to a perspective on singleness and marriage you may not have considered before.

Though singleness has been my gift and calling in life, God has walked with me in my journey as a single woman, and taught me some things I could not have learned on any other path. This book tells a part of that story.

My desire and prayer is that as you read this book, you will come to know God more fully and discover a new joy in your journey, whether single or married.

Exploring God's Purpose

The Single's Choice

Therefore a man shall leave his father

and mother and be joined to his wife,

and they shall become one flesh.

GENESIS 2.24

chapter one

WHEN ARE YOU GOING TO GET MARRIED?

Both of my parents, of Swiss descent, grew up in large Amish families during the Great Depression. My father had ten siblings, and my mother was one of twelve children. I am a blessed woman indeed to have come from a traditional family that has produced more than a hundred first cousins!

In the past, many of our holidays were spent either at my grandparents' place or a relative's home. The houses almost burst their seams trying to contain all the noise, people, and food. I recall one such occasion when we were gathered at my aunt's house. We had just finished washing mounds of dishes following a sumptuous meal when I joined some of my aunts and cousins who were chatting at a table. The direction of the discussion soon turned toward marriage and the latest dating couples. In my traditional Amish background, marriage and family are of utmost importance.

Suddenly Aunt Kate[†] turned toward me and said, "Sharon, just when are you going to get married?" Well, in that moment I was wondering too! I was already in my late twenties with no Prince Charming appearing on the near horizon. All eyes

---

† Many names in this book are fictitious to protect the identities of those involved.

turned toward me expectantly. Startled and somewhat flustered, I replied lamely, "I don't know; I have to get my siblings married off first." Maybe Aunt Kate sensed my uneasiness, for the conversation was soon steered elsewhere.

The question "When are you going to get married?" may have been addressed to you too. This question has haunted many young people, older singles, and widows. It is not always asked by others; more often the unmarried lady asks it of herself. I find it amazing that in our postmodern day, when many families are no longer intact and traditional family values have been discarded, most people still hope and dream of a marriage that will promise a lifetime of love and happiness.

What is it that makes every little girl (and even big girls) wistfully dream of being Cinderella with a glass slipper who will be found by her prince? What draws men and women toward love and commitment? Why do people cohabit even if they choose not to marry? And if they choose not to cohabit, why do some still engage in a promiscuous lifestyle?

Is there something so basic about God's original plan that whether we choose to believe in God or not, we instinctively know that men and women were created not to walk alone, but in relationship with each other?

TO MARRY OR NOT TO MARRY

The first time I recall being made aware of my single status happened during a brief interview for a teaching position in a local Christian school. After the formal interview with the board, the pastor was expected to close the meeting. He began reading aloud from a section of Galatians 4 for the closing comments. Suddenly verse twenty-seven crashed into my consciousness as the pastor read, "'Rejoice, O barren, You who do not bear! Break forth and shout, You who are not in labor! For the desolate has many more children than she who has a husband.'"

Confused, I wondered, "Why ever is he reading this passage? Is he thinking I am not going to get married?" In that moment, I concluded it had something to do with my acceptance of the teaching position as a young woman in her twenties. I did not recognize the prophetic tone of those words, or I probably would have fled from the interview.

I doubt I shall forget the Sunday morning when my uncle walked across the church aisle to shake my hand. I was in my early thirties, but I had never expressed to him any desire for marriage, so his comment took me by surprise. "Sharon," he said, "I have been impressed to share something with you. If you want to get married, I encourage you to really, really pray about God bringing you a husband." He spoke a few more encouraging lines. I nodded in agreement, trying to process his unexpected exhortation, and the conversation soon ended.

My mind was spinning. Where did trust in God's ways, and my demand for marriage and family converge? Although I was desirous of such a gift, I didn't want to pray for something I would later regret. Neither could I discern whether my motives were pure and unselfish in asking for the gift of marriage.

Then there was a time when I was in my upper thirties that one of my extended family addressed my singleness in a most surprising way. My uncle Glenn and his wife Lizzie lived out of town, and needed a place to stay overnight. I offered them my bedroom.

The next morning they thanked me profusely for sharing with them in this way. They generously wished me God's blessings. Next, Uncle Glenn closed his eyes and prayed a short prayer that God would bless me with a husband. Stunned, but deeply moved, I thanked him for his kind words. We never discussed my desires for marriage and family, yet he was willing to risk speaking into my singleness.

Why did these people, who knew little about me, feel compelled to address my marital status? Were those God-moments? Other single men and women have heard similar words. Something feels out of sync when one is single. Unmarried people are perhaps a reminder that something is not quite like it should be in this world.

WHEN IS IT MY TURN?

As a young girl I dreamed of getting married someday. I suppose I was quite normal in that respect. My mother married when she turned twenty, and why would it not be the same for me? In my upper teens and the decades that followed, I kept wondering the same question Aunt Kate posed to me: "When are you going to get married?"

The first time I really tangled with the tension of singleness and marriage was a warm, balmy day when I was sitting on a green lawn in an Ozark valley. I had been a student at a Bible institute for a few weeks. I felt many stirrings as a young lady in her late teens interacting with a fine group of young men and women. I deeply longed to move into the realm of romance and courtship.

That afternoon I wrote out on a piece of notebook paper some of my life desires and my life commitment before God. This paper certainly included the deep desire for marriage and family as well as my commitment to follow God whether single or married.

During my twenties, my journals reflect many low periods in my life. Although I was the oldest in my family, my younger siblings were getting married. I kept teaching in our local private school because nothing better turned up. I was biding time until marriage would whisk me out of the classroom and I could get on with life. It didn't happen.

I struggled with discouragement and depression. Reflecting on that time, I should have shared with my family my internal conflicts. However, heart conversations can feel awkward, and very few people thought to pursue me this in area. Additionally, my tendencies leaned toward introspection, and I processed best by thinking and writing. Hence my journal became my closest confidant in those days. As I recently reread some of these journal entries, it became obvious that I was grappling with the tension of being single.

In my early years of singlehood, I never heard anyone say that my longing for marriage was a natural, God-given desire. I assumed I needed to be content in my singleness and not desire too much. I also assumed it was more spiritual to desire single life than to desire marriage. More than once I berated myself for the lack of maturity I demonstrated in being dissatisfied with my single status. After all, wasn't the fact that no one had asked me proof that this was God's will for my life? I felt guilty that I was not content with being single.

As I approached my thirties, I recognized that marriage

and family were beyond my ability to make happen. Four of my siblings were all married before the age of twenty-five. That left two of us siblings at home. I was still hopeful that marriage might arrive on my doorstep after I was attracted to a fine man in his thirties. I prayed and hoped that our friendship would grow. I waited and waited. By the time I turned thirty-eight, my eighteen-year-old sister was seriously dating a fine young man, but no man was coming to see me.

One night I vented my anger into my journal. I peevishly wrote, "Lord, I can't believe it has happened to my sister before it happened to me. She has been asked, and I still have not been asked. I wonder, doesn't faithfulness count? I have tried to be everything You want me to be. Yet never have I in all these years been chosen as a wife. Sure, people say, 'You have a ministry to touch lives,' but what about my dreams? What does it take, Lord, for You to grant me the desires of my heart?"

February of 1995 I entitled my journal the "Black Hole Month." In it were many dark, dreary entries. I could not make sense of my singleness and my sister's gift of courtship. One evening toward the end of that month, despair barged in with all its fury. Although I dearly loved my youngest sister, I resented her bubbly excitement about the budding relationship with her man.

I was feeling quite sorry for myself by bedtime and concluded that I'd had a rotten day. I started crying in my pain of loneliness and deferred hope. Hot tears spilled down my cheeks. I was angry that God had not come around to me on the basis of my "goodness" and provided a husband. At some point those angry tears turned to brokenness as the Holy Spirit began convicting me of my pettish demands that insisted God must come through on my terms. Something broke inside me that night.

Slowly it dawned on me that God was not compelled to come through for me on my terms. The simple, profound truth is that God is God. Anything He chooses to do is His prerogative, and what I receive from His hand is purely the gift of grace. My heart turned toward repentance. This perhaps was the first time that I truly began embracing the disappointment and reality of my singleness. Strangely, this also began the process of my acceptance and healing. Not everything changed overnight. Neither did it obliterate my desires. I still had hard days and dark journal entries, but slowly my self-focus began changing to a God-focus.

Many women I know have not chosen their status of singleness. The gift of singleness has been placed into their laps. How do we reckon with the deep desires and the unanswered questions we have as single women? To give us a foundational perspective of our singleness, let us briefly consider two life questions.

THE QUESTIONS THAT TAKE US TO THE BEGINNING

First we need to ask ourselves, "For what purpose was I created?" Was it to get married and have a family? Is that the sum total of life? The second question is even more important, "Who is God?" Why did He create humanity in the first place? How do singleness and marriage fit into His plan?

Most of us enter life in pursuit of one thing—our own happiness. Watch any newborn baby, any toddler. Not one person has to be taught the art humanity is so naturally good at: forcing the world to revolve around ME.

Unfortunately, even as adults we may approach life situations from this standpoint. What is best for me? What will make me happy? While we would hesitate to make a grand statement that life is about our own joy, we quickly become uncomfortable with the idea that it is not!

Before we delve too deeply into the questions surrounding marriage and singlehood in our pursuit for happiness, let's look at the bigger picture of God.

GOD IS

Who is this God who set humanity upon a spinning sphere in the universe? I remember the day as a youngster when I first became overwhelmed with the idea of an eternal God. As I sat at the table enjoying lunch with my siblings, I began asking my mother where we came from. Through a series of questions and answers, my mother informed me that our first parents were Adam and Eve. My next question was, of course, "Well, where did they come from?"

My mother replied simply, "From God."

This led inevitably to another question—the big question—one that I suppose every child with the knowledge of God will ask sometime in his life. "Where did God come from? Who were His mom and dad?" I wondered aloud.

"God always is God. He had no parents," my mother replied.

I recall in that moment bogging down with the profound simplicity of her answer. In my young mind there had to be a beginning, a point in time when God began. Who formed Him? Where did He begin? Who could have birthed Him? Why didn't He have a father and mother? What if there was a time without God?

Infinity baffles our limited comprehension. We cannot know everything there is to know about our own lives and planet earth, let alone God's eternal existence. In every way, we are less than He is. Our strength, our beauty, our longevity, our accomplishment, our righteousness, is nothing compared to His. Yet this great God in His infinite loving plan created you and me. We are His image bearers on this earth by His design and for His purpose.

CREATED FOR HIS PLEASURE

While God intended man to reflect His likeness and carry a part of His Spirit, God also created us for His pleasure. John caught a glimpse of this truth when he saw the twenty-four elders worshiping their Creator in heaven and crying out, "'You are worthy, O Lord, to receive glory and honor and power; for You created all things, and by Your will they exist and were created'" (Revelation 4:11). Overwhelmed by their recognition of God's purpose in creation, these twenty-four elders, redeemed men of dust, prostrated themselves and worshiped.

The Almighty One's pleasure is not just a warm, fuzzy feeling that has espoused us to Him. Rather it is (in the active sense) His "choice, purpose, [and] decree,"[1] setting into motion a creation to bring Him glory, honor, and power. We were made specifically for His purposes alone.

If you were a child in the 1960s, you remember drive-ins. I sure do. An A&W Root Beer drive-in was located on the edge of our small, rural town. My family frequented this place for cold drinks on warm summer evenings. As my father chose a parking spot under the long carport, a teenaged carhop came to our open window. My father placed the order, and we eagerly anticipated the frothy soft drink! After some time, the carhop returned with a tray of frosty root beer mugs. Ah! That first glorious sip from an ice-cold mug was delightfully sweet. It tingled all the way down our throats. For a little girl who rarely had the luxury of soft drinks, it was a moment of pure pleasure. In that moment, my heart longed to burst forth expressions of gratitude for my father's kindness and love.

As a young child, I was totally dependent upon the kindness of my father's heart to give me something I could not acquire on my own. He was the superior, producing a moment of joy, and I was the subordinate, participating in the gift of pleasure. Although it was a temporal, physical pleasure and remains only in memory, the participation of a subordinate with the superior is analogous to the scene in heaven with the twenty-four elders. The subordinate, the created ones, moved in oneness with the purpose of creation. They could worship the Superior because they understood their utter dependence upon Him.

God, too, calls our hearts to participate in this way and to submit to His purposes for our creation and for our lives. He longs for hearts that choose to worship Him with lavish praise and honor for His sovereignty.

THE HAUNTING QUESTION

By now you may be saying, "Why bother asking questions about God and humanity's purpose on earth when we are discussing singleness and marriage?" You may wonder why God doesn't change your marital status if He is powerful enough to create the world. We want God to provide according to our expectations and desires.

However, the fact remains: God is the "I AM." He is the center. We need to recognize and accept that humanity is not the focal point of creation. We must rather acknowledge the One who is, and turn our praise and worship toward Him regardless of our circumstances.

Until we clearly understand and accept God's power and love—in His creation of humanity and His Sovereign purposes for this world—we will live shallow and disappointed lives as women, whether single or married.

How do we understand and accept God's power and love as single people? Do we have the same value as do married people? The next chapter will attempt to answer these questions as we go back to the beginning, when God placed the first single man and the first single woman on the earth.

chapter two

ALONE AND A SINGLE RIB

I most often have felt alone as a single in social settings. I prefer not attending formal events such as dinners, celebrations, weddings, or funerals by myself. That may sound strange because social events imply the presence of people. Why then would my aloneness be heightened during those times? There may be a few reasons. It requires additional energy to make social rounds in formal settings alone. Sometimes I recognize very few people, and I don't always know how to initiate comfortable conversations. Social events often suggest paired seating. This can be awkward.

I recall one such incident when I attended a dinner with my family a number of years ago. After the hostess put the dinner on the table, she and her husband began seating their guests. My parents were seated. Next my married siblings, along with their spouses, were seated. Unfortunately, by that time the table was full, leaving only enough room for the host and hostess.

The hostess looked at me apologetically and wondered if I would mind sitting with the children in the kitchen, where she had already set me a place. I can't say I had very gracious thoughts at that moment. I did not exactly feel validated as a mature woman in her upper twenties. And that was not the only time it happened. I have had a few similar experiences, even beyond my twenties. (I must admit that those experiences were character building for me.) The bottom line is that we do not always know what to do with people who are single.

Unmarried people sometimes evoke negative stereotypes in our minds. We envision a skinny spinster with a sharp, pointed chin and a wart dangling from her nose. In our minds, gossipy old maids make it their business to know everyone else's business. We read stories of unshaven, unkempt bachelors living in dilapidated bungalows with their one-eared mutts. We picture a stooped-shouldered hermit living in a hut on the mountainside, entering civilization only for his yearly trip to town. Repulsed and appalled, we cry, "Lord, deliver me!"

Single people have been around for eons; in fact, they began at creation. Why did God begin by forming a man to live alone, and then, in what appears to be almost an afterthought, create a woman? Why did God not speak a married couple into existence? He could have done that!

Who were these first single people, and what was God's initial purpose for them? How were they designed spiritually, physically, and relationally before God brought them to each other? What were their tasks in God's creation? Perhaps we will not be able to satisfy our insatiable appetite for in-depth answers, but let's explore the creation account for some possibilities.

ADAM: A SINGLE MALE

Chapter one of Genesis gives us a chronological account of creation. The story begins with day one and ends with a completed creation on day six. God spoke, and the world came to be. While each day held its own miracle of becoming, the sixth day held astounding detailed activity. On this day, the Creator's creativity reached its zenith. God not only formed the wild and domestic animals, but also created man in His image and likeness.

God, the Trinity, spoke within Himself to form a spiritual being made in His image and likeness. In stating His plan, God used the plural pronouns *us* and *our*, indicative of the Trinity, when He said, "'Let Us make man in Our image, according to Our likeness'" (Genesis 1:26).

So the first male was created, and his name was Adam. Adam was an eternal being with an eternal destiny. The preacher in Ecclesiastes 3:11 described it this way: "[God] has made everything beautiful in its time. Also He has put eternity in their hearts, except that no one can find out the work that God does from beginning to end." The living soul within Adam was the basis for connection with God. Adam could now respond to his Creator with choices, ideas, and worship.

Adam was not only spiritual, but also physical. Maleness was more than just anatomical and physiological differences from the female. God created masculinity at the very core of Adam's being. In this, his manhood caused him instinctively and fearlessly to pursue, initiate, dominate, and subdue.

God placed Adam in the Garden of Eden, giving him two specific jobs concerning his masculinity and leadership. Adam was instructed to *tend* the garden and *keep* the garden (Genesis 2:15, emphasis added). As a man, he was to engage in meaningful and purposeful work, serving God.

Work in the Garden of Eden was not meant to be a hardship, but rather a fulfilling, exhilarating adventure. Adam's service in the garden became an act of worship to his Creator. Adam worked with purpose and freedom, and without the cumbersome weights of boredom, irrelevance, and futility. He was instructed to step into his sphere of influence with confidence and courage.

Adam's masculinity and leadership were further confirmed by God's second charge to him, to be a "keeper" in the Garden of Eden. As a keeper, Adam was called to protect and guard against anything that could bring harm to his realm. The word *keep*, *shamar* in the Hebrew,[1] has the connotation of guarding both offensively and defensively. Adam was expected to guard defensively and establish boundaries to guard offensively.

Adam was also created as a relational being with volitional capacities. Adam's first taste of a relationship was with his Creator. God communicated presence and expectations. He showed Adam everything he could eat, but also told Adam the one thing he must not eat—fruit from the Tree of Knowledge of Good and Evil. Adam, as a single male in the garden, was learning how to face daily confrontation of choices while working in the garden, caring for the garden, and eating from the garden.

Living in the Garden of Eden, Adam had no other person to distract him from knowing and loving God. He appeared to have the perfect life. God had provided him with all the physical comforts of food and home. Adam had a meaningful job and a purposeful calling. He managed and protected the Garden of Eden, a flourishing greenhouse. He had dominion over the beasts of the field and the fowl of the air. He was the man in charge, with no uprisings to threaten him or challenge his leadership. In addition to all this, Adam experienced perfect unity with the God of the universe. What more could he need or want?

Yet it was not enough. Adam could not fully recognize his human potential and capacity while living in the garden with no one like himself. To learn, grow, and develop as a person, he needed another—like himself and yet unlike him. He needed someone who could affirm his strengths and expose his weaknesses. This could not occur in his single state. God revealed Adam's aloneness. He said, "'It is not good that man should be alone; I will make him a helper comparable to him'" (Genesis 2:18). Adam's masculine humanity would be tested at the very core in relationship with another human.

ADAM: IN SEARCH OF ANOTHER

The earth began in a state of sinless perfection, with nothing lacking before the Fall. However, earth's perfection did not cancel the need for growth and relationship. Something was lacking for Adam, and this void was not good. Adam lived in a world much larger than himself. He needed someone to assist him in his work, production, and ruling.

But even more basic, Adam needed someone to complete him. He was not self-existent. He needed someone who could fully reveal both his potential as a male and God's purposes for him. Although God recognized that it was not good for Adam to be alone, Adam also needed to recognize this.

God took a rather amazing route to help Adam discover his need for another. He set him on a quest that led him to the revelation of his incompleteness. God brought the animals to him and "whatever Adam called each living creature, that was its name. So Adam gave names to all cattle, to the birds of the air, and to every beast of the field" (Genesis 2:19-20).

So committed was Adam to this task of naming the animals that he didn't stop until it was completed. However, after naming the animals, Adam was gripped with the stark realization that he was alone. (He had given something *from* himself by naming the animals, but not *of* himself.) We then read the first profoundly disappointing words in Scripture: "But for Adam there was not found a helper comparable to him" (Genesis 2:20).

What were Adam's thoughts and ideas as he named the animals, but did not discover a helper suitable for him among them? Imagine with me for a moment how this might have happened.

Adam tingled with excitement. The creatures were gathering about him. The Voice spoke. "Name these creatures, Adam. I am bringing them to you to name, and perhaps you will discover for yourself a suitable helper."

Adam began, "Elephant, lion, giraffe, zebra, gorilla, camel…"

The Voice interrupted. "Are any of these a likely helper, Adam?"

Adam smiled wryly. "No," he replied shaking his head, "they are strange and awesome creatures, but I can hardly imagine one of them as a suitable helper." Adam continued his task, "Cow, horse, dog, kitten, robin, crow, butterfly, snake, lizard, frog…" So the time passed, with Adam naming animal after animal.

Finally Adam paused. He named the birds, the domestic

beasts, and the many animals that now surrounded him, but where was a suitable helper among them? They were not of himself or like himself. Had he missed something in the task? Slowly he turned his broad shoulders, now slightly stooped with weariness, and walked toward the cypress tree.

A Voice stirred the breeze. "A job well done, son. Though you have named the creatures, you have not found a helper suitable for you. This alone is My task, son. She needs to come from a part of who you are and of who you are not. So great is this mystery of fashioning a suitable helper that it can only be done by My wisdom." The Voice paused and continued. "Adam, are you willing to enter the deep darkness of waiting while I take from your side a rib to fashion one like yourself?"

Startled by this question, Adam pondered briefly before replying. "My Creator, I don't know about darkness, but I long to have my helper fashioned in the glorious light of the Creator. I trust your wisdom and plan." Adam closed his eyes. Suddenly a profound darkness swept into the very fabric of Adam's being. Adam opened his mouth, drew a deep breath, and slumped into unconsciousness.

God tenderly beheld the man before Him. Adam, His son, was now going to discover a part of himself he had never known before. He grasped Adam and rolled him over. Placing his hands firmly upon the rib cage, the Creator opened Adam's side. The healthy tendons and muscles were tightly wrapped around the ribs. Smiling, the Creator decisively broke off one rib with its flesh still attached. Closing the exposed side, the Creator began forming. Time passed. Adam slept in the darkness while God worked in the light. Eventually, the Creator paused; His work was almost completed.

A still form lay before Him. He bent down, imparting life to her heart. He saw her chest rise and fall as her heartbeat thudded softly and steadily. Slowly she opened her eyes and beheld the intense love of her Creator. God smiled.

A helper suited to Adam could not come out of a vacuum. She would have to be a part of Adam himself. Her creation required of Adam a deep, death-like sleep—a sacrifice of his own life in order to bring another into existence. Author Nancy Groom wrote why she considered this deep sleep significant.

> It was not man's human initiation but God's that brought the woman into being. The man's contribution was his "death," his deep sleep. He had to "die" and suffer the loss of an intrinsic part of himself for God to bring the woman to life, setting the pattern the Apostle Paul would later describe in Ephesians 5 as a husband's sacrificial love.[2]

Adam did not find his suitable helper by searching, but rather by submitting to God's idea for his counterpart.

God had spoken into this single man's aloneness. Loneliness and aloneness are not synonymous. One can feel the rush of loneliness whether standing alone or standing among thousands of people. Aloneness, however, is simply the state of being alone. Aloneness for a time can be healthy and refreshing, but total aloneness is devastating. Alone and without a helper, Adam's spiritual, physical, and relational dimensions could not be fully realized.

THE WOMAN: FROM A RIB

What paradigm could best symbolize the idea of suitable helper? God didn't open Adam's head and use a part of his brain to form a helper suited to him. She was designed to be more than an intellectually stimulating counterpart or an equal in leadership. Neither did God cut off a part of Adam's hand to create a suitable helper for him. Hands symbolically facilitate independence and power. Nor did God slice off a part of Adam's foot. His helper was not intended for mere servitude to respond to Adam's every beck and call. And she did not come from Adam's shoulder, to match or supersede his muscular strength and ability. Instead, God touched the most vulnerable part of Adam—his side—in the breaking of a rib. The helper came from near his heart and lungs: the place of God's life-giving breath.

Like Adam, the woman God formed needed a spiritual dimension. How did she receive the life-giving breath and become a living soul? We do not read that God breathed into her as He did Adam. He may well have done this. But could it be possible that her soul was already intrinsically wrapped and animated in Adam's when the Lord God imparted life to him? Genesis 5:1-2 (KJV) offers some provocative thoughts in relation to this idea. We read,

> This is the book of the generations of Adam. In the day that God created man, in the likeness of God made he him; male and female created he them; and blessed them, and called their name Adam, in the day when they were created.

The question remains—how much of the woman's being was already a part of Adam before she was created as his helper? Let's explore this further. Word studies indicate that the noun *likeness* in the Hebrew language is in the feminine gender, and the noun *image* is in the masculine gender. Does the use of this word *likeness* in verse one indicate that this female was already a part of the man when God created him? Could her soul have been present in the creation of Adam's soul? The creation account is rather obscure in the details of creating the first woman.

However, we do know one thing. Clearly from the time of the woman's creation, the writer in Genesis made a decisive distinction between the two as male and female. Adam was fully male. The woman was fully female. They were not the same even though God "called their name Adam" (Genesis 5:2 KJV). Though created to be joined, they were now two separate entities, two living souls, whose reuniting could happen only by choice.

THE WOMAN: WHAT ADAM LACKED

"Who am I, Creator?" she asked.

"You..." the Creator paused. "You are the crowning touch to creation. You came from man, and you are created for man. You reflect the glory of man."

"How do I reflect this glory?" she asked.

The Maker smiled. "Man needs one who can come alongside him and do what he cannot do for himself. You will accomplish this purpose with your beauty and your understanding, but most of all with your love. Your love will be more than romanticism—instead, a love that will sacrificially give its very life for the sake of the beloved, who is powerless to accomplish his calling and purpose alone. Are you willing?"

The woman felt a deep stirring within and quickly responded, "Show me the one, Creator."

"Follow Me," replied her Creator.

The single woman stood, and together they walked through the midst of the garden, where grew the Tree of Life on one side and the Tree of Knowledge of Good and Evil on the other. Perhaps in that moment God sorrowed. He knew what the woman did not. Before long, she would succumb to the Tempter's voice and break her commitment in the delusion that she could live independently of God and her husband. Eventually the woman and her Creator reached the one called Adam. By all appearances he was sleeping.

"Stay here," the Lord God whispered. The woman knelt beside the sleeping form. She waited, silent and curious. Captivated by the pulsating life and beauty of the garden, she smiled. Touched by the life and love in the garden, the Woman rested and waited. Time could be no enemy in a place where there was total harmony.

Adam stirred. His eyes slowly opened. He tried to remember, shaking his head to clear his foggy brain. Where was he? What had happened? Something had changed, but what? "Oh, yes!" Adam touched his side. A helper! Where was she? Suddenly he caught a whiff of jasmine. Adam sat bolt upright and turned.

There she sat a few paces away, gazing at him with luminous eyes and a tender smile curving her mouth. The wavy tresses cascading down her shoulders intertwined with sprigs of white jasmine. Her slender hands gently reached forth, inviting the man before her. Awestruck, Adam rose slowly. He had never seen a more dazzling creature! Intoxicated by her beauty, he moved effortlessly toward her.

Firmly grasping her soft, warm hands, he pulled her up toward himself. In that moment Adam knew that she was his completion. "Woman," Adam whispered, looking into her eyes. Then he cried out jubilantly, "'This is now bone of my bones and flesh of my flesh; she shall be called Woman, because she was taken out of Man.' Therefore a man shall leave his father and mother and be joined to his wife, and they shall become one flesh" (Genesis 2:23-24).

We don't have historical evidence of this imagined conversation. Much of the story remains a mystery. We do know the woman was not to work independently of this man, but in connection with him; for indeed, she was a very part of who he was. She was also an individual created with the capacity to make life choices. What she did for Adam would be her gain, and what she did against him would be her loss.

Adam, too, made a declaration of this unity and individuality. We read that he declared the woman to be "bone of my bones and flesh of my flesh" (Genesis 2:23), referencing her origin and their shared likeness. Then he gave her a title of her own: "She shall be called Woman, because she was taken out of Man." The word *woman* is a beautiful play on words in the Hebrew language—the *ishshah* (female) coming from the *iysh* (male).[3]

As the woman rejoined her husband, they expressed God's image and likeness together. How all this was brought to completion, we may not fully grasp. But we do know that the woman shared Adam's spiritual dimension and life-giving capacity, for they were made in the image and likeness of God.

THE WOMAN: HER COMPLEMENTS

What help could the woman offer Adam? First, she could join in his daily responsibilities for the productivity of the garden. Her intelligence, creativity, ideas, and encouragement enlarged the garden with even more possibilities. What Adam could not see, she could see. What he could not do, she could do. What he could not feel, she could feel. What he could not envision, she could envision. That is the beauty of the marital union. Such a union does not come about in a moment, but is cultivated over a lifetime. "We grow one as our goals become the same, and as we labor together toward those goals, helping one another."[4]

Recall our earlier discussion of Adam's role as guard and protector of the garden. How was he to do this? Certainly he could put some physical boundaries around the garden, but was there more? Could it be that the woman's intuition would also serve as an unseen boundary? A female's intuition is intrinsic to her. She discovers it at a very young age and carries it into adulthood.

I recall the day this was vividly illustrated in my classroom. We were reading aloud from our current novel, *Amos Fortune: Free Man*, by Elizabeth Speare. The plot peaked when Amos, the protagonist, discovered that his wife Violet had taken money matters into her own hands. She had hidden his hard-earned money, which he had planned to give away instead of using it to purchase their land. As Violet sat facing the land, she sensed that Amos was standing in the doorway. At this point, I paused the reading. I asked the students if they understood and experienced that "sense"—the intuition Violet had in that moment. Of my twelve fifth- and sixth-grade girls, eleven knew precisely what I was talking about, but not one young man in my classroom could identify with the sense of intuition!

Many times a woman's intuition senses imminent danger. Thus Adam, who was called to protect the garden, might have been grateful many times for the assistance of his helper's intuition.

Next, the woman, as his 'help meet' (Genesis 2:20 KJV), became the welcome counterpart to Adam's masculinity. He could not fully experience his manhood and productivity without a 'help meet.' She was so like him and yet so unlike him! He needed the help of someone different from himself to fill the emptiness of what he was not. She brought to him the beauty, gentleness, and goodness of life itself. She made him fruitful and dynamic. In knowing her, he could know himself.

This woman, the 'help meet,' could participate in the man's daily duties surrounding his life calling. And yes, she could mirror his differences and complete his masculinity, but there is more! She was created to support and aid his leadership. Ultimately their union was to expand God's purpose and design as created beings.

Adam was called to subdue the earth, rule over the animals, and make physical and spiritual provisions for his family. Before the woman was created, God gave Adam instructions on what he might and might not eat. He had all the information he needed for sustenance and life. But it was after God introduced the Tree of Knowledge of Good and Evil that He said Adam needed a suitable helper. Adam could hardly have grasped the implications of his choices if he were alone. His choices would have affected him only. Could he have understood his potential to sin and his need for God if there was not one to challenge his leadership?

This single woman, too, was incomplete without the man. The purpose for her creation—the very essence of her womanhood—was clearly defined. With this man, she would procreate and carry the fruit of their union. She was created to long for connection with the man from whom she was formed. She was to be loved and cherished in the oneness they would share.

We started with two single people in the garden, each with a specific calling and purpose as they merge into oneness of spirit, soul, and body. One is called to initiate a relationship of unity, and the other is invited to enter the relationship in support of that union. Theirs would be a perfect blending untainted by sin, a union in which a male and female who had been single became one flesh.

chapter three

FOR THIS CAUSE

My cousin, a dreamy-eyed bride in white, sat chatting with her bridesmaids and toying with her long-stemmed pink roses. She still had a few minutes before it was time to enter the church auditorium and celebrate this momentous occasion in her life. Suddenly, she looked around with awe and murmured incredulously, "I can't believe this is happening to me. It was always someone else getting married, and now it is my turn!"

Undoubtedly, most brides have similar thoughts of wonder. To be sought out, to be chosen, to be loved, is miraculous for any woman. And she anticipates that the miracle of love will cause her to live happily ever after.

I suppose almost every little girl dreams of growing up and walking down the aisle as a bride. Little girls instinctively understand that they are destined to become wives and mommies. It doesn't cross their minds that it will be otherwise. The truth is that not every little girl ends up married. She may remain single for reasons unknown to her. By the time she grows up, a girl may even have lost her desire to marry.

A woman's tender heart can be deeply hurt by the harsh realities of life. Though destined from the beginning to be a help meet, she sometimes disdains the very thing for which she was created. If she is single and does not embrace her potential as a help meet, she soon scorns the beauty of this calling and becomes a hard, angry woman. If she marries, she soon realizes that marriage is not the fairy tale she imagined it to be. Her husband is disappointingly flawed—a man standing in need of God's grace. She often fails to realize that she, too, brings sin into the relationship. Carolyn McCulley writes, "Marriage is a blessing, but it's also a lot of work. It's two people committing to love and forgive each other for the rest of their lives, to the glory and honor of God."[1] Both wife and husband daily stand in need of God's grace.

In the beginning, according to Genesis one and two, marriage was God's plan for mankind. Included in this plan was His design for a female help meet in the marriage union. The Apostle Paul clarified this idea in I Corinthians 11. He wrote, "[the] woman is the glory of man. For man is not from woman, but woman from man. Nor was man created for the woman, but woman for the man" (11:7-9). Although God created the woman for the role of help meet, He allows her to choose to embrace or reject His design. Embracing this role beautifies the mystery of her femininity; rejecting it shames her at the core of her femininity.

One may wonder—what is so grand or glorious about a marriage in which a woman is confined to a subservient role as help meet? Does the woman need to surrender her personal dreams and budding career for the sake of another's goals and aspirations?

Many women in American culture and the Western Church ask similar questions. "Why does the woman need to set herself aside and live in the shadow of her husband? What about her dreams? Her goals? Her personal fulfillment?" Such questions expose an improper understanding of God's purposes in marriage. He intends to bring wholeness to two people as they function together in their God-given roles. While it may look like a "subservient" woman narrows her life considerably, life lived in pursuit of her own pleasure and fulfillment leads to the worst narrowing of all. A woman who allows her own needs and desires to dictate her life will someday face the reality that her happiness and realm of influence have shrunk; her heart has hardened. God knew what He was doing when He asked us to live for the glory of another.

THE UNION OF MALE AND FEMALE

It seems rather surprising that Adam's vital, spiritual relationship with God was painfully inadequate for him as a man. God said that Adam needed another person to complete him. Why? Remember, only God is complete in and of Himself. He is the essence of love and needs no person to bestow His love upon. Men and women cannot love sacrificially or even romantically unless there is an object upon which to impart their love.

This first marriage was not based alone on romantic feelings. While they undoubtedly experienced strong romantic attraction for each other, the premise of their marriage was based on connection and completion, requiring sacrificial love to keep the union unbroken and undivided. The strength of the marriage union lies in its intimate connection, which reduces humanity to its most basic nature and, at the same time, pulls the heart and soul to unimagined heights.

Imagine how Adam's strong voice cried out with joy as he made the remarkable discovery of his wholeness when the woman took her place at his side. He said, "'This is now bone of my bones and flesh of my flesh; she shall be called Woman, because she was taken out of Man.' Therefore a man shall leave his father and mother and be joined to his wife, and they shall become one flesh" (Genesis 2:23-24).

Without hesitation, Adam declared his connection to the woman and her completion of him. Immediately following the declaration, he explained the result. He said man would leave his parents and be joined to his wife so that two could become one. This was not just an idea Adam made up. He was echoing God's design for mankind. Adam faithfully passed on God's plan as a directive for generations to come.

Jesus, too, confirmed that this marriage idea came from God. In a discussion with the Pharisees, He said, "Have ye not read, that he which made them at the beginning made them male and female, and said, 'For this cause shall a man leave father and mother, and shall cleave to his wife: and they twain shall be one flesh'?" (Matthew 19:4-5 KJV).

From Adam's declaration we see that marriage is a union of connection and a union of completion, as two people become one flesh. We will briefly examine these two purposes of marriage as stated in Scripture.

A UNION OF CONNECTION

Connectedness in marriage is a process and takes a lifetime, but "leaving" is an initial choice. Leaving requires a physical and emotional relinquishment of one's past security. For a woman, it is the first step in trusting her man to protect and provide for her. For the male, it is the choice to physically leave his former place and exercise his leadership responsibility in the establishment of his own home. The leaving is not only physical; it is also an emotional severing. A woman must break the emotional ties of loyalty that have subjected her to obey the wishes and desires of her father. Emotional and physical relinquishment of the former life is vital if a man and woman are to experience soul connectedness.

Some women (and men) see marriage as an escape from dysfunctional homes or relationships. They gladly leave the physical place that has brought them pain. They incorrectly assume that physical distance will also create emotional distance. That is not true. Unhealthy or negative emotional ties will trail people into their marriage union regardless of the physical distance. Couples must reckon with the importance of breaking negative emotional ties in order for true connectedness to occur in their marriage. When a woman's bitter emotions keep her tied to her former life, she is limited in oneness and connection with her husband. She is being mastered by the co-dependency of her conflicting emotional ties.

A marriage relationship struggles to survive in the context of divided loyalties produced by unresolved emotional issues from the past. Anything that controls your heart can also divide your heart. If the past controls your heart, it will become a greater focus than your marriage. Jesus taught a principle of this dichotomy concerning heart loyalties. He said, "'No one can serve two masters; for either he will hate the one and love the other, or else he will be loyal to the one and despise the other'" (Matthew 6:24). You cannot stay loyal to your marriage and the past with equal commitment. Only in choosing the path and process of forgiveness can you leave a dysfunctional home or relationship that has mastered you. This opens the door to freedom and wholeness in your marriage.

Refusing to let go of a painful past is not the only deterrent to "leaving." Sometimes men and women idolize the security of their parents and former home. They hang onto their safe past and struggle to leave behind what they have experienced as good. In doing so, they unconsciously hold back a part of their heart in the marriage union. For a woman, this is especially true if she perceives her husband to be incompetent. It is necessary for a woman to be willing to leave what has been safe and good—and with faith and trust join her husband in the adventure of building oneness in their new home.

Connectedness in marriage is about leaving one thing for the purpose of joining to something else. Joining is an action the King James Version calls *cleaving*. "Therefore shall a man leave his father and his mother, and shall cleave unto his wife" (Genesis 2:24 KJV). The Hebrew word for cleave is *depaq* which means to "impinge," or in the figurative sense "to catch by pursuit."[2] Synonymous to *impinge* is the word encroach, literally meaning "in hook"[3] with something.

Cleaving is the entwinement of soul and spirit in ways that

are only appropriate in a marital relationship. It is the commitment to stay emotionally connected and intact. It is to "stick fast" and to "stay attached,"[4] to be hooked without any other viable options. In Adam's declaration, the cleaving seems to be the responsibility of the husband; however, unless the wife turns toward her husband with a trustful heart, the man cannot find entrance into her soul. Without a *cleaving* connection, two fragmented people will live in the shell of marriage rather than in the spirit of marriage.

We have looked at the prerequisites for connection, but what happens as the result of this soul union?

Connectedness blesses a marriage with companionship—a relationship in which each partner blesses and affirms the other. In its earliest forms, the word *companion* meant "one who eats of the same bread."[5] In Scripture, eating together often symbolized a covenantal relationship of two souls. It then is not surprising for a single to most keenly feel her aloneness when she sits at a table with no one to break bread. It is also not surprising that we feel most comforted when we sit at the table with a good friend in mutual agreement. How much more then should eating together in the covenantal relationship of marriage allow connectedness to deepen as we partake of the same "bread and wine"?

Connectedness fosters intimacy—the deep companionship that cries out to know and to be known. Each learns to sense what the other feels and knows without speaking a word. We were created for such intimate fellowship; it is the cry of the soul. When we experience intimate companionship, we know that God has come near. Amos 3:3 cries out, "Can two walk together, unless they are agreed?" There is no companionship-connection if there is no agreement between two spirits.

Connectedness not only offers companionship and intimacy, but also rest. A close union offers peace to the hearts of both husband and wife. Yet we may wonder how, since marital connection can never be perfect. If two people in marriage cannot stop working at their relationship, what kind of rest does marriage offer?

Rest in marriage may look slightly different for the husband than for the wife. In discussing the virtuous woman, the writer of Proverbs shows how a husband can be at peace. "The heart of her husband safely trusts her; so he will have no lack of gain" (Proverbs 31:11). The husband's rest has everything to do with the kind of woman he has brought to himself. If she is a virtuous woman, he can rely on her, confide in her, and trust her. His rest is a "firmness or solidity"[6] that comes from complete confidence in his relationship with his wife. In this deep connectedness, a wife brings honor to her man and rest to his heart.

Similarly, the woman who is joined to her husband in spirit is a woman at rest. At her husband's side, she has found a place to belong, and in belonging she finds rest. Naomi recognized this truth when she told her two daughters-in-law goodbye in the land of Moab. She encouraged them to leave off following a bitter, old woman, and instead to "'find rest, each in the house of her husband'" (Ruth 1:9). She wanted her daughters-in-law to be consoled in their losses and find rest in their homes.

Orpah did return to her homeland, but Ruth clung tenaciously to Naomi and Naomi's God. Ruth understood that her route to rest was not through retreating into the security of her past, but in leaving it and cleaving to a mother-in-law who served Yahweh. Ruth now had a companion and a home. Naomi, however, understood the struggle and inadequacy of two women living alone. Female companionship can be right and good, but it can never offer the soul-and-spirit connectedness of marriage. At its best, it is still inadequate in providing the rest that results from marital union. One day Naomi said to Ruth, "'My daughter, should I not try to find a home for you, where you will be well provided for?'" (Ruth 3:1 NIV).

Woman was not created to live alone. Within every woman is an ardent desire for connectedness to someone. A woman's lack of connectedness results in restlessness. I have talked to restless married women who are not connected to their husbands. I have talked to single women who put their lives on hold, waiting impatiently for the connectedness they long to experience. Both single and married women tell me they long for the physical and spiritual protection and security of a good man. But underscoring all of that is the deep desire to belong to someone.

A UNION OF COMPLETION

Besides providing connectedness, marriage also celebrates completion. Two separate lives, two separate souls, and two separate hearts become complete in the union of marriage. Adam had no doubt that this woman fulfilled what he lacked, for she was indeed of his bone and flesh. No one person is a complete sum total in himself, or herself. Each needs another to fill the void of that which he lacks. How does this completion occur? How is the emptiness filled?

For a visual picture of completion, imagine assembling the interlocking pieces of a jigsaw puzzle. Now, we know from experience that only one puzzle piece will fit in one place at one time. Sometimes we pick up a piece whose color and shape deceive us into thinking it would be an exact fit. But unless it is the exact fullness of the other's emptiness, it will not interlock. The puzzle can be completed only when what was empty is joined by the precise fullness it lacked.

Both husband and wife bring into marriage limitations of capabilities and personalities. Both spouses also bring into marriage the fullness of what they can offer in these areas. This makes it possible for two different individuals to merge into the completion of oneness.

Sometimes women panic when they think of merging into another's heart, will, and life. Merging into oneness requires surrendering one's own identity to establish a new identity together. Most women want the blessings and benefits of oneness, but are reluctant to pay the price of surrender that such a union requires. In a broken world, hearts can slide their interlocking puzzle pieces in and out of marriage based on personal advantage or convenience. This deeply affects the union of completion. If one chooses to pull completely away from the interlocking oneness, devastating results follow.

Jesus understood this and spoke against it. He said, "'Therefore what God has joined together, let not man separate'" (Matthew 19:6). In the spirit of grace and the new covenant, this teaching goes far beyond the physical separation that divorce brings. Marital oneness means connection in spirit, soul, and body. This is the completion Adam referenced when he said that man and woman were now one flesh. In giving to and receiving from each other, their similarities and differences complement the beauty of their union at every level.

How is the completion of two people complementary to who they are? Often the chemistry of like interests draws them together. They may share the same ideas, tastes, goals, ministry, or hobbies. This is what I call complementary completion. An art student is not in class very long before he learns the concept of adjacent shades on the color wheel. Adjacent hues enhance artwork. Likewise in a marriage, the commonality of interests and ideas often blends into a harmonious relationship. The pleasant similarity, coupled with the diversity of female and male perspectives, enriches the wholeness of this union. Together, the man and woman delight in sharing themselves with each other. Marriage as a union of completion celebrates the discovery of each other. The exhilarating discovery of similarity should lead to union, not competition, between the spouses.

Did Adam fully understand that his unity with the woman also involved contrast? Perhaps the first clue we have of Adam's ambiguity about their difference comes during his observation of her dialogue. He appears uncertain of what to do while his woman engages in conversation with the crafty serpent. She is the one talking, not Adam. She participates in an intellectually stimulating conversation with spiritual overtones. She longs to experience all that is available.

In this interchange, we can attempt to contrast some of the differences between the man and the woman. The woman engaged in conversation, but Adam kept silent.[7] The woman longed for something elusive, while Adam apparently wanted to leave well enough alone. The woman was seduced by a spiritual imposter; Adam didn't respond. The woman was deceived into eating fruit, but Adam knew what he was doing when he chose to join her in it. What happens to a union of completion when the disparities surface? Can a man and wife truly be one in the face of contrasting differences?

No one individual has all the strengths and capabilities needed to survive in this world. In marriage, a spouse offers not only a pooling of strength and ability, but also dissimilar aspects to complete what each is lacking. A marriage that has no differences is a shallow relationship, indeed! Yet too often we allow our personal differences to spark relational struggles. We are threatened by what the counterpart has and defensive of what we have not. We begin engaging with a subtly competitive spirit instead of honoring and accepting what each has to offer. Remember, the "puzzle piece" can fit only if it has a different cut.

Again, take the example of a color wheel. The *beauty* of the wheel lies in its adjacent colors, but the *power* of the wheel lies in its contrasting colors. The intensity of these contrasting colors—red and green, blue and orange, yellow and purple—is so powerful that sometimes they seem to vibrate when placed side by side.

In the same way, contrasting differences in relationships call forth responses. Can we learn to appreciate the beauty of contrasting colors in relationships rather than feeling threatened? Differences require humility. In a marriage, differences obligate both spouses to receive with gratitude what the other spouse offers. That is why, whether married or single, we need community. No one person has it all, and humility blesses the completion that differences bring.

Completion in marriage not only celebrates similarities and differences, but also through them serves a procreative purpose. Offspring is propagated by the union of the two. The physical differences of male and female make it possible to submit to God's purposes for reproduction. One of the Lord God's first instructions to man is found in Genesis 1:28. He said, "'Be fruitful and multiply; fill the earth and subdue it.'" One spouse cannot act independently of the other to fulfill this command.

God intends that procreation happen in the context of marriage. Reproduction as He commanded is both a physical and spiritual act. In a man and woman's oneness of completion, life is transmitted. This certainly reflects the oneness of the Godhead and His longing to reproduce sons and daughters. When His Son became human and tasted death—a physical act—He also transmitted life by giving Himself—a spiritual act. His goal was "bringing many sons to glory" (Hebrews 2:10). In the context of marriage, reproduction is a sacred expression of the union's completion as God intended.

The union of completion and connection is the foundational basis of any marriage, according to Genesis 2:23-24. Adam understood that his completion came in joining to another, like him and yet unlike him. Their souls, their hearts, their bodies, their wills, and their minds connected with a depth that is only possible in marriage. "Feminine is good and masculine is good, and both together are even better."[8] Cleaving brought connection to Adam, and oneness brought him completion; but was God's design for marriage broader still?

GOD'S INTENT

*And he answered and said unto them, Have ye not read, that he which made them at the beginning made them male and female, and said, **For this cause** shall a man leave father and mother, and shall cleave to his wife: and they twain shall be one flesh? (Matthew 19:4-5 KJV, emphasis added).*

Why did God institute marriage in the beginning? Let's step away for a moment from the first two chapters of Genesis and look at Scripture as a whole story. God began the world with a marriage, and He will end the world with one as well! In Genesis we have the first marriage account between man and wife; the last marriage is found in the book of Revelation. When Christ returns He will marry His bride, the Church. God has placed a premium on marriage. He could have filled the earth with people some other way. He could have spoken every human being into existence. He could have allowed people to temporarily cohabit for reproductive purposes, like the beasts of the earth, but He did not. God designed marriage to reflect the union of our eternal destiny.

Throughout Scripture God shows Himself in the context of relationship. He is in relationship with His creation, and with Himself through the Trinity. He longs to be in relationship with those whom He created in His image and likeness. However, after sin entered the world, it tipped the scale toward evil, and men lived in broken relationship with God. Evil escalated before the Flood. It reached its peak when the "sons of God came in to the daughters of men and they bore children to them" (Genesis 6:4).

Such mingling did not produce godly marriages of completeness and connectedness. Humanity defied the purpose God intended. To cleanse the earth of its wickedness, God sent a flood and destroyed the world.

After the Flood, God entered the earth in a more personal way. He chose a friend, a man called Abraham, and his descendants, the Israelites. God knew Abraham would be faithful. He said, "For I know him, that he will command his children and his household after him, and they shall keep the way of the LORD, to do justice and judgment" (Genesis 18:19 KJV). God chose this people to further reveal His purposes for the world. He longed for His love to be reciprocated, so He espoused Israel to Himself. He spoke through Moses, calling His people to "'love the LORD your God with all your heart, with all your soul, and with all your strength'" (Deuteronomy 6:5).

True to human nature, the Israelites apostatized, grieving the heart of God. Again and again He reminded them of the union He longed to share with them. He called Himself Lover and Husband in wooing His people. "'For your Maker is your husband'" (Isaiah 54:5).

> You shall no longer be termed Forsaken, nor shall your land any more be termed Desolate; but you shall be called Hephzibah [my delight is in her], and your land Beulah [married]...For as a young man marries a virgin, so shall your sons marry you; and as the bridegroom rejoices over the bride, so shall your God rejoice over you (Isaiah 62:4-5).

God pleaded with adulterous Israel, saying, "'Return, O backsliding children'... 'for I am married to you'" (Jeremiah

3:14). God promised that if they turned from their apostasy, He would make a new covenant with them. "'It will not be like the covenant I made with their forefathers when I took them by the hand to lead them out of Egypt, because they broke my covenant, though I was a husband to them'" (Jeremiah 31:32 NIV). In that day of the new covenant, the Lord God said, "'I will betroth you to Me forever; yes, I will betroth you to Me in righteousness and justice, in lovingkindness and mercy; I will betroth you to Me in faithfulness, and you shall know the LORD'" (Hosea 2:19-20). God longed for a relationship with His people that would parallel and even surpass the connection and completion He intended for earthly marriages!

The marriage theme is also woven throughout the New Testament. John the Baptist introduced the idea of Jesus' coming as a Bridegroom. John clarified that he himself was not the Christ, but "'the friend of the bridegroom'" (John 3:29). Why did Jesus begin His public ministry at a wedding? Could it be indicative of His identity and the cause for which He came? Later, when Jesus was asked why His disciples did not fast like the Pharisees, He compared Himself to a bridegroom, replying, "'Can the friends of the bridegroom mourn as long as the bridegroom is with them?'" (Matthew 9:15). On another occasion, He taught the disciples how to anticipate and prepare for the eternal marriage. In a parable, He told them to live with the anticipation of a bride, and to prepare themselves as a bride expecting her bridegroom (Matthew 25:1-13). Jesus was likening His final appearance to that of a husband coming to receive His bride, the Church.

The marriage theme continues in the Epistles. The Apostle Paul, writing to the church at Ephesus, included marital instructions to love unconditionally and sacrificially. He encouraged husbands to love their wives as Christ loved the church. He explained that Jesus literally gave His life for His church so that she might be one with Him. Christ longed to "present it to Himself a glorious church, not having spot or wrinkle or any such thing, but that it should be holy and without blemish" (Ephesians 5:27). This marriage will surely be a union of completion and connection in its purest form! Paul referenced what was said in the beginning, "'For this reason [cause] a man shall leave his father and mother and be joined to his wife, and the two shall become one flesh'" (Ephesians 5:31). Paul grappled with trying to make his point adequately—for he concludes that one cannot explain its depth—and summarized by saying, "This is a profound mystery—but I am talking about Christ and the church" (Ephesians 5:32 NIV).

We move on through Scripture and come to Revelation, in which the Apostle John records his visions of the final marriage. Here we get a sneak preview of what is to come! The awe-striking scene unfolds in heaven as a great multitude begins shouting praises and honor to the Lord God Almighty. The voices of the multitude hit the highest decibels, comparable to the roar of rushing water and peals of thunder. In the midst of this celebration, they shout, "'Let us be glad and rejoice and give Him glory, for the marriage of the Lamb has come, and His wife has made herself ready'" (Revelation 19:7). Then an angel proclaims, "'Blessed are those who are called to the marriage supper of the Lamb!'" (Revelation 19:9).

We see God's heartbeat for humanity most clearly when we begin understanding that marriage was "for this cause." Earthly marriages reflect divine glory and design.

While we have looked at a few passages in Scripture on God's desire for marital intimacy with His people, we also see this purpose demonstrated by His Incarnation. God ushered in a New Covenant in the person of Jesus Christ, the second Adam. How was he different from the first Adam? The first yielded to temptation; the second resisted temptation. The first Adam blamed his wife for the sin; the second Adam took upon Himself the blame of sin. The first Adam failed in the Garden of Eden; the second Adam triumphed in the Garden of Gethsemane. The first Adam brought death; the second Adam brought life. The first Adam was unfaithful in his commitment to God and his wife; the second Adam is forever a faithful Bridegroom!

HOW DO SINGLES FIT IN THIS CAUSE?

When a man and woman marry, they reflect what God intended in the beginning. He wants an intimate relationship with those whom He has created. He longs for the same kind of connection and completion with His bride, the Church, as He designed to occur in an earthly marriage. Can married people more clearly understand God's desire toward us than single people can? Author Anita Yoder writes:

> I haven't experienced the incredible, mysterious waves of love and acceptance that a bride receives from her beloved. In a way, nothing compares to that radiance and beauty, and sometimes we singles feel as if we're missing a delightful feeling and experience. We are missing out, to a degree. And

> *yet, in the deepest sense of perfection [completion]*
> *and acceptance [connection], all of us are already*
> *chosen, loved, and cherished by a Person who wants*
> *to spend the rest of eternity with us.*[9]

I believe it is true that married people experientially know a level of oneness that singles do not. Their marriage union manifests most beautifully God's intent for completeness and connectedness, possible only in the context of such a relationship. The question remains—if God has placed so much emphasis on marriage, was it His original design that every man and every woman enter into marital oneness?

We find ourselves squirming under this idea. We would be much more comfortable saying that marriage was meant for most people, but surely not for everyone. We find it far easier to trust that it is God's will that some are not married than to believe that His will has not been accomplished. Our limited perspective of an infinite God moves us toward simplistic answers. We don't know what to do with a God who is larger than life. Our definitions feel safer and more manageable. We find it difficult to untangle a world that stands in need of God's redemption. How might it have been had sin not entered the world? How would marriages be different?

Suppose—just suppose—that perhaps God did intend every man and every woman to experience "that two should become one flesh." Suppose it was His highest good for mankind that every man and woman should experience a measure of completion and connection through the marriage union. Do you find yourself reacting to that possibility? "Well," you might exclaim, "if it is true, WHY IN THE WORLD ARE THERE SINGLE PEOPLE?"

chapter four

WHY IN THE WORLD
ARE THERE SINGLES?

A lovely young lady sat on my couch, twisting her fingers nervously as she talked. She found her heart attracted to a godly young man, but he seemed to treat her no differently than any other young lady. "I want so much to get married and have a family," she sniffled through her tears. Then looking apologetically toward me, she wailed, "I don't want to be single the rest of my life! How can I make him want me?" I gave her space to vent the frustrations that had built up within her. When she paused, I asked her a question.

"Do you really," I probed softly, "*really* want to get married?" She looked quizzically at me and slowly nodded. "I think so," she replied, puzzled.

"Why do you want to marry?" I inquired.

Her face brightened and with dreamy eyes she whispered, "I want to be loved."

I smiled and gently asked, "Are you more in love with the idea of marriage than you are willing to make the commitment to love in the way marriage requires?"

"What do you mean?" she challenged.

I continued, "After every wedding begins the reality of marriage. Marriage is two people's lifelong commitment to becoming one. It necessitates that both merge their agendas, their goals, and their identities for the sake of the marital union. The goal in marriage is not to seek love for one's self. Rather, you commit yourself to love your spouse sacrificially. Sacrificial love does not demand anything in return, even though it longs for love."

With downcast eyes she spoke hesitantly. "I never really thought about it that way. Maybe I was captivated more with the idea of being loved." Distressed, she looked up. "But where do I go from here?"

We talked together at length about the commitment of love and marriage, and God's purposes for her life. Toward the end of our time together, I asked her again, "Do you still want to get married?"

"Yes," she replied with certainty, her eyes glistening with tears, "but I am willing to wait for God's timing and direction."

I smiled encouragingly and said, "Your desire for marriage is of God. It is a good desire. Marriage is a part of God's design for completeness and connectedness. Pray and commit your life to Him. He will bring to pass the desires of your heart." We prayed together, I hugged her, and she left my apartment smiling.

QUESTIONS THAT MAKE US PAUSE

Why did this lovely young lady feel such an intense desire for love and marriage? Was this something she conjured up in her mind, or was her desire implanted by God? When God created the world, did He intend His creation to be evenly paired? Did He originally intend every man and every woman to walk to the marriage altar? Did the Fall of man impact God's original intent for singleness and marriage? Am I single today because Adam and Eve tasted the fruit? Or perhaps because of my own fallen nature? Does God call some people to be single and others to be married?

A large percentage of singles are unmarried for reasons unknown to them. Do we dare suggest it may not be God's perfect will that they are single? We don't like the ambivalence of this possibility, but let us think a bit more broadly. Is a dysfunctional marriage God's perfect will? Of course not! Can a person be in God's perfect will within that dysfunctional marriage? Absolutely! Are God's purposes marred in disappointing circumstances? They need not be. Could it be possible it is not always God's perfect will that one is single? When we take into account human choices and our fallen world, we have to say yes. However, can that single person live in God's perfect will? Yes!

Why doesn't God fix the single woman's marital status if singleness is not His perfect will for her? Let us jump back to the marriage analogy. Does God suddenly appear on the doorstep and wave a magic wand to fix a dysfunctional marriage? He does not! Sometimes He divinely intervenes in a situation. More often, He chooses to bring resolution through people's choices and life circumstances. Why should it be any different for the single person?

Many people sense that there is something a bit odd about not being married. Single life can feel like trying to fit a square peg into a round hole. Singles don't fit the norm. In a paired world, singleness may at times feel dysfunctional. I have lost track of the number of times people have sidled up to me or written me a note wishing me a husband and marriage. Why do they make such comments? Could it be that these people are agreeing with God's intention for mankind? Do their comments highlight the fact that singleness requires resolution, or at least an explanation?

God said that Adam's aloneness was not good. He spoke this truth while Adam was in the Garden of Eden. Everything in the garden was operating at the highest level of harmonious perfection, yet something was lacking. The aloneness of man in the garden cried out for completion and connection. How much more is this needed in our fallen world today? People were created to be not only in relationship with God, but also in relationship with each other. Marriage was designed to fulfill God's plan for human intimacy and fruitfulness. Further, marriage was intended to reflect His glory and love. So we return to the plaguing question, "Why in the world are there singles?"

JESUS' VIEW ON SINGLEHOOD

One day Jesus' disciples overheard Him discussing marriage and divorce with the Pharisees. The disciples were shocked that Jesus taught against divorce except in the case of infidelity. They suggested to Jesus that singleness was by far the better course if divorce was not an option in marriage. Jesus countered their conclusions by giving them only three reasons why one should consider singleness as a lifestyle. He said,

> *"All cannot accept this saying, but only those to whom it has been given: For there are eunuchs who were born thus from their mother's womb* [God's sovereignty]*, and there are eunuchs who were made eunuchs by men* [circumstances beyond one's control]*, and there are eunuchs who have made themselves eunuchs for the kingdom of heaven's sake* [personal choice]*. He who is able to accept it, let him accept it" (Matthew 19:11-12).*

Although Jesus was undoubtedly referring specifically to the eunuchs of that day, I believe that, in principle, this passage applies to single men and women today as well. What was Jesus saying? We could derive from this passage three valid reasons why people remain unmarried. First, singles live under the mercy and grace of God's sovereign purposes and will. Next, single people encounter circumstances in life that limit and hinder marriage opportunities. Finally, some singles have made a personal commitment to remain celibate for the sake of the kingdom of God. Let's explore these ideas in more detail, taking them in reverse order, from most personal to most encompassing.

SINGLE BY PERSONAL CHOICE

One evening I overheard a conversation between two singles. Tara, an older single lady, challenged Dan, a man in his upper thirties, about his limited dating experiences. She found it disconcerting that he didn't date more often. She felt that as a man he had the choice to date at any given point in time. "Why don't you just ask somebody?" she challenged.

Dan shifted positions and gave a short laugh. When he answered, frustration laced his tone. "It's not that simple. Just because there are possibilities doesn't mean that I can do it, or that I am free to do it."

Tara remained unconvinced. "Surely," she countered, "all you would need to do is to make that first move. There are plenty of women out there who would say yes."

But Dan remained convinced that it was not so easy to enter a relationship based on the availability of females. He felt it also had to do with God's timing and call.

Sometimes we, like Tara, consider the opportunity of marriage to lie simply with man's choice. In our minds, Dan could enhance his situation any time he wanted to, by choosing to pursue a relationship. We as women may even envy or resent the free initiative of a man. If we feel bound to wait on a man's lead, but he reneges, we are "stuck."

Sometimes people make a conscious choice to remain single. Other times that choice happens by default. Still other times it stems from subtle vows.

Do single women have a choice in their marital status? I believe the answer is yes— single women can choose to remain single or to marry. Single women may feel inclined to react to such a radical statement. They may say, "Oh, but I'm a lady! I don't have a choice in the matter." I argue that all humanity holds within itself the great and terrible gift of choice. Is it not true that if a woman is desperate enough for something, she can compromise and force her wishes to come true? In her book *Single*, Marilyn McGinnis firmly states that "any girl who is willing to lower her standards can get married if she wants to."[1] In such cases, a woman feels that the degree of her desire justifies her actions. If it is true that a woman can make the choice to marry, she certainly can also make the choice to remain single. Why should one consider choosing singleness over marriage? Such a choice must be weighed by the motives of the heart. We read in Proverbs 21:2, "Every way of a man is right in his own eyes, but the Lord weighs the hearts."

NEGATIVE MOTIVES FOR CHOOSING SINGLENESS

Some women (and men) are single by choice, but for the wrong motives. Singleness may be rooted in a reactionary decision. Perhaps the decision was born out of a negative home environment or relationship. A person may determine never to let a spouse hurt them in the same way their parents hurt each other.

Women who have been deeply violated in male relationships often decide to protect their hearts at all costs. Their explanations can appear noble. They say, "I would rather be single than have a dysfunctional marriage and make children suffer for it." Or they may say, "If this is what men are like, I would rather remain single than let a man hurt me again." It appears reasonable to protect one's self or children from a future dysfunctional home or hurtful relationship. Our sympathies are aroused toward women who have been violated to such a degree. However, are such statements not subtly rooted in an angry demand to live life without the mercy and grace of a Redeemer?

These silent vows from past disappointments and hurts in male relationships lead them to promise themselves, "I will never fall for a man again," or "I will never let myself hope again." Such vows may shut down their desires for marriage, and cause women to turn toward the survival devices of self-protection. They ward off potential relationships with weapons of independence, manipulation, anger, or scorn. These weapons greatly limit marriage possibilities. Again, they demonstrate a lack of trust and faith in a God who redeems and makes one's way perfect (Psalm 18:32). A woman's hurtful past is not reason enough to close her heart toward marriage.

By nature, most women easily turn toward suspicion and fear, which brings us to the second wrong reason why we may choose singleness. We are not certain we can trust anyone not quite like ourselves. If we have any indication that a man might coerce us under the domination of his leadership, we flee out the back door. We not only fear living under the suppression of a tyrannical dictator, but we also distrust spineless, weak males who refuse to live courageously. We fear a future that does not guarantee perfection and happiness in relationships, so we stay strong and we stay safe. This is clearly illustrated in an encounter that author Nancy Groom experienced. She said,

> I once sat beside an attractive young woman on an airplane, and as we chatted, I noticed on her left hand an unusual ring. Upon a closer examination, however, I realized my mistake; what I'd thought was a ring was really a tattoo of a small rose, its tendrils wrapped around her finger to replicate a ring.
>
> When I asked her about it, she told me that prior to becoming a Christian she had committed herself

> to never being married because she didn't think
> she could ever trust a man. The tattoo on her
> left hand was a "wedding ring" symbolizing her
> marriage to herself.[2]

Christian women may scornfully say, "Oh, I would never go to that kind of selfish extreme." Perhaps we will never be guilty of such a blatant act. I wonder, though, how many single and married women have lived in the spirit of such a self-commitment. When a woman determines to trust herself only, she might as well wear the ring tattoo. Her commitment to self-protection is just as wrong as wearing the symbolic ring. God is not fooled. He sees our propensity toward distrust.

A woman's refusal to trust another person—who potentially could disappoint her—could be a wrong reason to remain single. This is especially true if it is born out of selfish demand for perfection and happiness on this side of heaven. Undoubtedly, there are those situations when women cannot trust because of past pain and abuse. These women need time to heal and learn to trust again. Both hearts, whether selfish or fearful, stand in need of God's grace and mercy in order to open their hearts to another.

Living independently for one's own sake could be a third wrong reason to choose singleness as a lifestyle. With all the opportunities abounding for education, travel, and career, it is more possible than ever for a single woman to decline marriage in exchange for freedom. Embracing the pleasures that independence offers is far easier than entering a union of mutual goals, purposes, and identities. Women sometimes fear that marriage will inhibit their lives, particularly their ambitions and careers. The twenty-first century

career woman can hardly bear the thought of living in the obscurity of her home, taking care of toddlers. Our postmodern world
does not treat women kindly who assume the role of homemaking
as a calling. It decries the woman functioning in those "restrictive"
confines. Voices suggest that she needs to look out for Number
One, and not let anyone hinder her from pursuing personal
dreams. Unfortunately, women who buy into such philosophies
miss the beauty of Paul's instructions to Titus concerning young
women. He encouraged Titus to teach women that they should be
"keepers at home" (Titus 2:5 KJV).

Finally, could a woman's prideful heart close off the possibility of marriage? We are sometimes too proud to give expression
to our desires for marriage. We refuse to allow our close friends
to see our deepest longings. Instead we couch our statements
with false humility: "If God brings me a husband—fine. If He
does not, it doesn't matter." Or, "If God didn't give me marriage
by now, then it must be His will that I am single." Sometimes
the statement is a bit more aggressive: "Since marriage hasn't
been my lot, I am not going to ask for it." In the past, I have
made similar comments which issued out of a complacent and
prideful heart. Do such statements suggest that one's marital
status is somehow God's fault? Sometimes we are tempted to
wrap our assumptions around blame rather than face the underlying problem of our hearts.

God has created women with a capacity for deep desires and
longings. What should we do with them? Jesus invites us to do
three things with desires. He said, "'Ask, and it will be given
to you; seek, and you will find; knock, and it will be opened
to you'" (Matthew 7:7). Does that include asking for the gift of

marriage? I am not promoting female initiation or aggression. Suffice it to say that this passage has everything to do with desire. Sometimes women become angry with life when no men pursue their hearts. This anger quickly turns toward blame. In their blame, they begin to demand resolution. God is not a puppet to be jerked about by their petulant demands.

We women sometimes ask God to move in the heart of a man we admire. We pray and pray that this man will initiate a friendship with us, but nothing happens. Then shame accompanies the realization that we have opened our heart toward marriage but it was not reciprocated by the man we admired. How we respond to the finality of such an answer is crucial to our spiritual health as single women. We can walk away with head held high, saying, "So be it; I will never ask again!" or we can yield our desires before God in continual brokenness. God longs that our hearts align with His purposes and plans for our lives.

We have addressed four negative choices that may lead to singleness: reaction to the past, fear of relationships, desire for independence, and pride at stake. It would neither be fair nor accurate to assume that a woman (or man) who would choose to pursue a career or single lifestyle is automatically independent, or proud, or scornful of marriage. Certainly it is possible for a person to remain single, pursue a career, and be good-hearted in the process. However, one should search carefully her motives for choosing singlehood above marriage.

POSITIVE MOTIVES FOR CHOOSING SINGLENESS

Only a small percentage of single people have consciously

chosen to live single all their lives. Most times these people felt a specific call to give their lives in service and ministry for the kingdom of God. They recognized that marital responsibilities could encumber or hamper the ministry, so they chose to remain single. They willingly laid aside their own desires for what they deemed was a wiser choice. Truly, this is a noble commitment. We honor such people. Choosing singlehood does not necessarily negate the desire for marriage; however, when God calls people to live singly, His provision of grace empowers them to do so.

Jesus did not discredit the conscious choice to remain single for the sake of God's kingdom. Rather, He affirmed such a choice. Sometimes God uses people or organizations to call singles to serve in a capacity that marriage would impede. This was the case for Jim and Elizabeth Elliot. As young people, they dated in college. But after graduating from Wheaton College, they parted ways. They did not know if or when they would see each other again. Each felt a strong personal call to foreign missions, but not necessarily to the same place. Though they loved each other, they willingly put their calling above their desire for marriage. To their surprise and delight, they both ended up as missionaries in Peru, South America. In time, God directed and confirmed their steps into marriage.

Serving for the kingdom's sake may not necessarily include a foreign mission opportunity. Sometimes a family member's need makes one consider singlehood. Perhaps a family member has a debilitating disease and requires additional support. Maybe a parent needs daily assistance, or a sibling needs care. We applaud the selflessness of a person willing to make a deep sacrifice for the needs of others. Our tendency is to think that single people were born with some special internal mechanism that makes them immune to the desire for marriage. But this is not often the case. Even godly single people are fully human. Could it be possible that these single people are even more fully aware of their desires than many who are married? Their very desire and ability to love enables them to think beyond themselves and lay down their life for a sister or brother. This is an expression of love in its purest form.

Choosing singleness so that one can serve with less distraction is good and honorable. This does not mean that one who is married loves God less. Neither does it mean that the unmarried person's ministry is more important and more spiritual. A mother who gives sacrificially in the obscurity of her home has just as much of a ministry and calling from God as does the unmarried woman working in the public arena. The difference between the two has to do with focus. A married woman's focus is to unite with her husband's purpose and goals, and serve God from their shared commitment. The unmarried woman's focus is to singly unite with God's purpose and call for her life and serve from that commitment.

SINGLE BECAUSE OF CIRCUMSTANCES

Many older single women are not without the desire for marriage, but marriage opportunities have not developed for them, for one reason or another. The lack of marriage opportunities can often be traced to an unfavorable circumstance or situation they encountered. Something did not work out, oftentimes beyond their power to change.

Sometimes a single woman becomes anxious as she grows older, increasingly aware that her body is on a biological time clock. If she wants any sizeable family, it seems crucial that marriage occur by the time she is thirty. Yet often life's situations work against her. We do not have to live long before we realize that opportunities are not equally balanced. Some circumstances lead easily to marriage and some do not.

FAVORABLE CIRCUMSTANCES THAT LEAD TO MARRIAGE

At the ripe age of twenty-four, I left Indiana to go to Virginia. I planned to spend a year in voluntary service, teaching and working with handicapped children. My dorm mate was a gal from Lancaster, Pennsylvania. Our personalities blended well, and Barb and I became close friends. She soon shared with me her recent broken engagement. She did not know whether marriage would be an option for her again or not. In her disappointment, she turned her heart in trust to God's provision and purposes for her life. When our time terminated, I encouraged her to return to Indiana with me. After some consideration, she decided to do just that. I was elated to learn that we would be working together as co-teachers that fall.

My friend Barb chose to go to northern Indiana, a place that she considered "flat and boring." Little did she or I realize the outcome of that particular decision! Our meeting in Virginia and her move to Indiana seemed circumstantial. Are circumstances God-ordained? You decide. In time, Barb began calling Indiana "flat but exciting" when toward the end of that school year, she began dating my brother. The following summer I was a bridesmaid at her wedding and hugged her as my sister-in-law! We all love such stories! Did Barb's choices and circumstances of breaking an engagement, meeting me in Virginia, and moving to Indiana lead toward marriage for her? Yes. But why do choices and circumstances not lead to marriage for everyone?

CIRCUMSTANCES THAT HAMPER MARRIAGE POSSIBILITIES

People face difficult circumstances in life. Physical factors that result in health problems, debilitating diseases, or limited use of body functions may hamper opportunities for marriage, although not necessarily. I think of a few women I know who married despite their physical handicaps. Becky had cerebral palsy from a lack of oxygen at birth. She was confined to a wheelchair and had little use of her arms, but she married and birthed two children. Jean, who was engaged to be married, ended up in a tragic accident. Her spinal cord was injured, and she became a paraplegic. A number of months later she married her fiancé and since has given birth to a few children. Brenda, a young college student, became critically ill when her blood vessels hemorrhaged one night. There was hardly a spot on her body as big as a quarter that did not have a black and blue spot. She ended up having both of her legs amputated. Time passed, and she married.

We enjoy these delightful stories of single ladies who incurred physical limitations, yet married. They were loved by men who were able to see something that went beyond physical appearance or limitation. Does that mean that physical problems never hinder one from getting married? No, many times these problems do hinder marriage possibilities. Entering marriage is a greater responsibility for the healthy spouse when there are physical limitations. Many people are uncertain that they have the emotional and physical stamina to shoulder this extra responsibility.[†]

Closely related to physical factors is a woman's physical beauty or attractiveness. This is always a sensitive issue for a woman. One of her greatest fears is that she is not beautiful enough for a man to be attracted to her. Women learn early in life that external beauty turns the male head more quickly. Did you ever notice that it doesn't matter how arrogant or haughty a gorgeous woman is, she never lacks a passel of admirers? Yet the plain-looking woman with a gentle, quiet spirit receives barely a glance. Is that the fault of the male? When God made the man, He created him to see with his physical and imaginative eyes. It is simply the way God wired him. Man was created with an innate attraction to female beauty. Women spend billions of dollars yearly for beauty aids. Why? Women long to be beautiful, and men want them beautiful. A woman who is not physically attractive does not as quickly attract the men's attention.

Another circumstance limiting marriage opportunities for single women may be geographical location. Attending a small church with few or no single male peers limits the opportunities for marriage. There is always the possibility that if she had been from a community with more single males, she may have married. Geographical implications are also tied to ministry

---

† Most people are aware that any physical problem could occur after marriage, but the lifelong challenges of a physical disability can make one more hesitant to commit to marriage.

involvement and circumstances. Single women sometimes spend their prime marriageable years serving in remote areas with limited interaction with single men. It is possible that marriage may have come to them if they had been in another place.

Finally, we face the serious situation of an extremely close youth group or singles group thwarting marriage possibilities. Technology cultivates group closeness. Transportation and communication have made it possible for people to interact in ways they never did fifty years ago. Until the early 1960s it was rare for young people to leave home during the work week. This automatically maintained a healthy distance and mystery between the sexes. But distance is no longer a problem. With increased evening social activities in both schools and churches, young people seemingly have bonded more as a family than as a social group. This shreds the mystery of seeking a relationship with someone special.

Because of technology, social connections are no longer confined to planned activities. Today's technology pierces into private lives. We can be accessed at any time, any place. Young women and men can connect hourly through instant messaging via computer or cell phone.

These institutions, activities, and technological communications with the same people over a period of time breed familiarity. Free and easy interaction can soon build among the participants the kinds of relationships that should be reserved for immediate family. Some singles' groups or youth groups boastingly say, "We are as close as brothers and sisters. We are all one big family." One by one the fellows move on in quest of a marriage companion, while that same church abounds with single women wondering, "Where have all the good men gone?" My response is, "Who wants to date a sibling?"

What should a single woman do about her circumstances— health issues, beauty, geographical placement, and desensitized youth groups? Should she invest excessive amounts of money into restructuring surgeries for some physical malady or flaw? Should she move every few years until she has found her mate? Should she find a different singles' group or church? Changing her situation or circumstances will not necessarily change her marital status. The answer for godly women is to turn to the Lord in disappointing situations.

The Proverbs writer offered wise words for single women to consider. He wrote, "In all your ways acknowledge Him [the Lord], and He shall direct your paths" (Proverbs 3:6). There are times when God prompts a single woman to change something about her present circumstance. If He does, she needs to walk in obedience to His voice. At the same time, we must realize that our circumstances rest in the hands of the Lord's divine providence and sovereignty. A woman is created not for a life that revolves around her wants, but around a higher purpose, as we shall see in our next section.

SINGLE BY GOD'S SOVEREIGNTY

One day, the blue eyes of my five-year-old niece gazed up at me with a question. "Aunt Sharon," she asked, "are you a mommy?"

"No," I said, hugging her.

"Why not?" she asked.

I sighed, and wondered how I could simplify this answer for a five-year-old. I quietly replied, "I don't have a husband. I am not married." Satisfied with my answer, she hugged me and ran off to play.

Other people, too, have wondered why I am not married. Certainly I never imagined at eighteen that I would still be single at fifty. As a young girl playing with my dolls, I dreamed of being a mommy someday. While in my teens, I anticipated the day Prince Charming would appear on my doorstep. I entered my twenties putting life on hold, not wanting to dream beyond the marriage possibility. No, I am not single because I took a vow of celibacy.

"So, why are you single?" you may ask. If I would answer, "I am single because it is God's perfect will for my life," I can almost see you nodding in agreement. Secretly, you feel relieved that I am accepting and embracing my single status with spiritual maturity. Of course, I feel piously justified as I explain my life in one short sentence. But suppose the answer cannot be so compressed? Could it be that a number of life choices I have made have limited marriage possibilities for me? Probably. Could it be that circumstances inhibited my marriage opportunities? Perhaps. Could it be that in God's sovereignty I am single for reasons I do not understand? Undoubtedly.

John Coblentz, in his book *Christian Family Living*, suggests what believers should understand about God's sovereignty in relation to marital status. He wrote,

> *[One] blessing of viewing God's sovereignty as
> large enough to permit the flow of human history,*

and the exercise of human choice, is that it gives
us the freedom to trust our lives to His goodness.
God is big enough to accomplish His will in the
lives of His people even while permitting the flow
of natural and human events. [3]

Could it be that my marital status is shaped by my life choices
and circumstances, and God chose to work within that limited
realm? I believe so. Does that mean God cannot transcend limitations? The answer is an emphatic "No!" God can do anything, but
He most often works within the natural laws and boundaries He
has created. Take the example of the earth's movement. We know
the earth spins on its axis, making one rotation every twenty-
four hours. Although God operates in and confines Himself to
the sphere of this scientific law, it does not diminish His sovereignty. God's infinite sovereignty enables Him to work His will
and purposes within His defined laws and boundaries.

God's sovereignty also enables Him to work with volitional
beings. We are not puppets dancing unconsciously to every whim
of our Creator. He is not pushing buttons and pulling strings on
us. He formed each of us with a living soul to think, choose,
plan, and worship. God wants His people to make life choices
and live courageously in them. Because He is God, He is able
not only to work His will within the realm of our choices and
circumstances, but also to transcend it for His purposes.

Sometimes we blame our situations, including our marital
status, on the sovereignty of God, when in reality the fault
may lie with us—perhaps on our own indecisiveness and un-
willingness to take personal responsibility for lifetime choices.
We would rather assume that what happens or does not happen

is God's fault. We often are hesitant to say it that strongly, so we soften it by tacking "the will of the Lord" onto our current situation. We say, "It is God's will that I am single, and there's nothing I can do about it." This attitude produces complacency and shallowness. Neither does it lead the soul to worship God. Such a statement never addresses the question of one's personal involvement. Subtly, the blame is shifted to God. Whether we want to admit it or not, where we are today has much to do with our personal choices and circumstances.

How then does God override this to accomplish His purposes? First, let's ask another question. How does God view this world? The Psalmist says it clearly in Psalm 24:1. "The earth is the LORD's, and all its fullness, the world and those who dwell therein." God's sovereignty demands that all belongs to Him. He has unlimited power and resources. He can orchestrate His purposes in any way He chooses.

Single people may not know why they did not marry, or why they lived singly for many years before they married. Jesus reminded the disciples that God, in His sovereignty, does permit people to remain unmarried. However, Jesus did not explain all the whys and wherefores.

It may be that some people are single primarily for God's own delight. He is a God who longs for undivided worship and devotion from His created ones. I wonder at times if God may intervene and hinder marriage opportunities so He can use single people for the advancement of His kingdom. Perhaps God directs people in a path of singlehood for a personal work He wants to do in their hearts that could not be done any other way. More maddening is the thought that I may be single for purposes which I may never know or understand this side of heaven.† That, too, is God's prerogative. In this, God calls us to trust Him in what we do not know or understand, for nothing is hidden from Him.

However singleness touches your life—whether you have never been married, are recently widowed or divorced, or find yourself in a disappointing marriage—all of us share a commonality of vulnerability. We were created for connectedness and completeness. We deeply desire the fulfillment of this reality. In our need, we face the temptation to chase after anything that promises to fill our hungry hearts. Unless we accept God's sovereignty, we will struggle to believe "that in all things God works for the good of those who love him, who have been called according to his purpose" (Romans 8:28 NIV).

Our bent is to be selfish and impatient. We know what we want, and when we want it, and how we want it. We want to know everything now, to get all the details figured out, and to get on with life. We despise waiting. This impatience shows up in single women longing for marriage, and it shows up in women already married. The single woman demands to know why God does not send her a husband. The disappointed married woman demands to know why God does not change her husband.

We resist the limitations of being human and living on earth with less than desirable circumstances. In our demand for relief, we seek a quick fix. We turn to Scripture to find a verse that

---

† Our finite minds do not have the capacity to understand everything God is working in this earth that will bring us to the consummation of all things. He is incomprehensible in His omnipotence and omniscience. How can we even begin to give definition to all the things we do not understand in the light of eternity past, present, and future?

surely will change our situation if we have enough faith. We cling to something like Jeremiah 29:11 and tape it to the mirror in our bathroom: "'For I know the plans I have for you,' declares the LORD, 'plans to prosper you and not to harm you, plans to give you hope and a future'" (NIV). We smile with relief, for we know these promises must include a husband if we are single, or be a sure sign of a changed husband if we are married. Often we are disappointed that change does not occur, and we become disillusioned.

But the essence of faith is not in taped messages, or in praying hard enough. Faith is understanding and believing that there is One who will override my purposes for His purposes alone.

Rarely do we wake up in the morning thinking about God's sovereign purposes. More often, we wake up thinking about how life will revolve around us. What if life and God's purposes are about something far greater than we can see? The fact is, we have a very limited perspective of God's overall purposes. We don't see the whole picture, and for reasons unknown to us, God does not bring good men to our doorsteps. Neither does He change our husbands. What then is our calling and purpose as disappointed single or married women?

Our general calling is to be human and bring glory to God—to delight in good food and be in awe of the rumbling thunder, to glory in what both point us toward. But what is our unique calling? It is to use (and be used by) our stories to tell the story of God. He has given us our unique set of stories to make something known about Himself, something that reveals His infinitely variegated being. We

must follow the path of our personal redemption to
understand the calling that we alone can answer.[4]

Who are we to say that God has made a mistake in orchestrating our life events? God does not owe you or me any explanations. The bottom line is that "I exist for God and for His purposes, not my own."[5] When I can embrace this concept, I can stop asking, "Why in the world are there singles?" and accept the reality, "Why, in the world there are singles!"

Singles will face unique challenges living in a world of married people. However, many of their challenges and struggles are not drastically different from those of their married peers. Singles have the same relational needs and frustrations as do married people. No matter what our status or situation in life, God calls us to care more about His will than our own and to trust Him for what we do not understand. The best praise we can offer Him is that of a life surrendered to His purposes.

Envisioning God's Plan

The Single's Identity

The Lord will give grace and glory;

no good thing will He withhold

from those who walk uprightly.

PSALM 84.11

chapter five

SHAME WEARS FIG LEAVES

By the time I was in my upper thirties, I had achieved my educational goals and developed a successful teaching career. I was actively involved in my local church and the larger community. Many of my friends and peers were married and in the middle of raising their families. Although I had seized many opportunities and held a promising career, I longed for yet one more thing. I would gladly have given up my teaching career in a heartbeat to become a wife and mother.

The summer I turned thirty-eight offered possibilities of life-changing events when I consented to join a mission team for two months in a remote part of the world. I loved the change of pace the summer brought! I entered into the cultural challenges and domestic responsibilities with much enthusiasm. This provided a welcome change from the routine of checking papers and preparing lesson plans. I knew little about this isolated place, but I was excited about its ministry opportunities. And soon after my arrival, I met "the man" who might change my life.

He was the kind of man I always had dreamed of meeting someday. Although he was tall and good-looking, it was his manly gentleness and quality of leadership that most attracted me.

Whenever I entered his presence, his friendly eyes lit up with recognition. My heart was strangely warmed, and I felt femininely alive. I responded easily to the conversations he initiated, and his kind words filled the hungry crevices of my heart. What more could I want as a woman? Before I knew it, I had opened my heart wide to the potential of this relationship developing into something more than a casual friendship. Summer came to a close, but my hope did not as I bid this man goodbye.

I returned home anticipating a phone call or a letter following our summer interaction. But time passed by with nothing of the kind. One afternoon as I walked out the school's front doors and down the sidewalk, I suddenly felt an overwhelming desire to hear some word from this man. Where was he? What was he doing? Would he make a surprise visit to see me? As the fleecy white clouds scuttled across blue September skies, loneliness squeezed my heart and tears surfaced. More weeks passed, and with them came a resounding note of silence.

Suddenly I realized what I had done. I had bitten from the fruit of desire, and now I felt the sting of that choice. I realized this man's silence meant one thing: he was not interested in a future commitment to this friendship. I vacillated between fury and disappointment—with myself and then with him. Other days I was engulfed in profound shame that I had allowed my vulnerability to be exposed. Oh, how I longed to run and hide! If only I could erase the man's name from my heart as easily as I erased names from the chalkboard! I felt I had played the fool not to see that he only intended it to be a mutual friendship and nothing more. My heart writhed in shame. Would I ever rise and be whole again?

THE ULTIMATE TEST

For many weeks I wallowed in crushed disappointment. Had my heart been so deceived by desire? In the disgrace of my vulnerability, I sought to hide. Whether single or married, perhaps you can identify with my vulnerability and shame, for we are all daughters of Eve. We desire pleasant fruit. We see good things. We are tempted. In our desire for fullness, we reach for things that promise fulfillment. Eating the fruit on that fateful day infected Eve's life with shame. We too, as her daughters, have felt the spiraling effects of shame in the choices we've made for ourselves and our relationships. Do we need to live in our shame forever?

Remember, the first woman's highest calling was to be a helper suitable for Adam. Adam was incapable of doing it alone, and his woman was designed to come alongside and complete what he lacked. She brought to their union an intuitive ability to expose evil, predict consequences, explain truth, and praise God and her husband.[1] Using these four feminine gifts, the woman could assist her husband in the productivity and protection of the Garden of Eden.

Eve had the intuitive ability not only to envision things that could nourish and bless their garden, but also to predict things that could damage it. Her intuition armed her to expose the dangers for what they were. She was competent in reasoning and articulating assumptions based on the truth she knew and understood. Finally, she brought honor to God and her husband when she turned her heart in grateful praise for their provision and security. It would seem that she was fully and perfectly equipped to aid man in his role as garden keeper. Sadly, neither Adam nor the woman reckoned with their power of choice.

The ultimate test came in a most surprising way—as a relational tension that jeopardized the union of connection and completion. In the hour of temptation, Eve, with her innate gifts, should have exposed the wily serpent. It appears she was the one who noticed him first. Genesis 3:1-5 gives us some insight into this initial conversation.

> *Now the serpent was more cunning than any beast of the field which the LORD God had made. And he said to the woman, "Has God indeed said, 'You shall not eat of every tree of the garden'?" And the woman said to the serpent, "We may eat the fruit of the trees of the garden; but of the fruit of the tree which is in the midst of the garden, God has said, 'You shall not eat it, nor shall you touch it, lest you die.'" Then the serpent said to the woman, "You will not surely die. For God knows that in the day you eat of it your eyes will be opened, and you will be like God, knowing good and evil."*

The woman was able to clearly state the consequences of death in partaking from the tree. She was also able to produce a truth-based explanation to the serpent as to why they were to avoid this fruit. "We are not to eat from the tree in the midst of the garden, lest we die," she informed the serpent. Maybe her simplistic answer felt a bit inferior in comparison with his wily reasoning. The woman attempted to clarify her point. She deviated from God's truth by adding her own explanation. She informed the serpent that they were not even to touch the fruit.

While this was probably a very good idea, it tampered with God's initial command. Her exaggeration led her away from a truth-based focus and took the first step along a slippery line of reasoning. At this point, the woman should have stopped and given herself into the care and protection of her husband. Unfortunately, she did not entrust herself to her husband's leadership in this dangerous conversation. Even though Eve confidently articulated her thoughts, she lacked a clear understanding of the situation. She focused on her environment instead of her husband and God. Unknown to her, she crossed a boundary line by engaging in a conversation that seemed perfectly harmless.

DECEIVED BY A SPIRITUAL VOICE

The woman's first step toward deception subtly yet effectively silenced her husband's and God's voices. The serpent's deceptive suggestion seduced her to defend their freedom in eating from all the trees save one. She felt compelled to fix the lie. She entered into a dialogue that by all appearances was quite innocent. It was a spiritual tête-à-tête that fully engaged all her sensory faculties and her vulnerable heart. Had the conversation been blatantly evil, surely the woman would have been suspicious. Duped by a spiritual imposter, the woman opened her heart to a misleading conversation. She never intended to turn away from God or sin against Him. Rather, she longed to experience more of God and His good intentions toward her.

Whether single or married, women today have the same propensity as Eve toward the spiritual domain. Churches generally have far more women than men. Why? Is it because women have a greater capacity for the spiritual, or because their hearts are more deeply hungry for God? Perhaps the real reason lies in the fact that women are easily enamored by promises of personal fulfillment when those promises are rich with spiritual overtones. Women are stimulated by voices that offer something beyond what they are presently experiencing. Often the deception is wrapped in subtle voices that sound harmless and insinuate both holiness and personal fulfillment. We gravitate toward voices that validate our spiritual inclinations and protect our vulnerable femininity.

What happened to Adam's voice in the garden? Why did he not speak up when the crafty serpent began engaging his wife? According to Genesis 3:6 he certainly heard the dialogue, because when the woman took the fruit, she also gave it "to her husband with her." His temptation came not from the seductive voice, but rather from the woman. Adam did not reckon with his wife's deep longing to become god-like instead of godly. Was he at a loss to know how to please both his wife and God? The woman desperately needed his protective covering. He had been commanded to "keep" the garden, and now their very souls were at stake. Perhaps he reasoned that there surely would be no harm in compromising a bit for the sake of his wife. Who would know? Most likely, Adam didn't want to disappoint his lady or withhold something from her that she longed for. So Adam compromised by his silence and willfully participated in disobeying God's command. 1 Timothy 2:14 discloses what happened in that moment. "Adam was not deceived, but the woman being deceived, fell into transgression."

Women endanger their lives, and the lives of those they love, when they shut out the voices of their primary men. By that I mean the men most closely related to them biologically. God places these men in women's lives to protect them from seductive voices. Singles need to honor the voices of their fathers and brothers. Married women need to honor the voices of their husbands.

Some women might say with horror, "Oh, but you don't know how cold and indifferent my primary man is. He has little or no interest in spiritual things." Yet he still has a voice, and God can use the primary man to protect the woman through her submission in honoring him. Unless his counsel transgresses God's commandments, his authority is her safeguard. Women who find themselves in the unfortunate situation of having a father or brother as a sexual perpetrator, or who are struggling in the wake of a divorce or separation, should seek a male family member who can offer spiritual directives.

Women should be slow to consistently seek assistance and advice only from males outside their biological family or marital domain. Men outside your family often have limitations in understanding the family dynamics. Those who have been constantly with you from your childhood and live with you know you better than anyone else. God can give to these primary men, whether they are Christians or not, a voice of wisdom and counsel to speak into your life if you choose to honor them in this way.

Fear, pride, or spiritual arrogance can hinder a woman from hearing the primary men God has placed in her life. As women, we should never disdain their counsel just because we assume they lack the spiritual or relational insight we have. Our tendency is to use measuring sticks that compare our men's level of spirituality with that of our female friends. "Because men's walk with God is often unlike our own, it's easy to dismiss their spirituality as inferior to ours."[2] While a male's spiritual journey may look different than a female's, we women need the balance of the male's perspective to keep us grounded in our spiritual journeys. Our submission to their words of counsel is, in reality, a covering of protection for our vulnerable hearts.

DECEIVED BY A SPIRITUAL VENEER

The woman's deception began when she listened to a misconstrued statement that planted a seed of doubt. In her attempt to rectify the serpent's obviously flawed statement, she created a moment of pause that allowed her heart to engage with all her sensory faculties. She was drawn up short by the intoxicating beauty and fragrance of the Tree of Knowledge of Good and Evil. What did she experience in that crucial moment? "So when the woman saw that the tree was good for food, that it was pleasant to the eyes, and a tree desirable to make one wise, she took of its fruit and ate. She also gave to her husband with her, and he ate" (Genesis 3:6).

Lest we judge this woman too harshly, all people are predisposed to cross boundaries for the allurement of beauty. Women have the capacity to appreciate and produce beauty. It is our supreme realm of influence. Beauty is one of the woman's greatest endowments, but unfortunately it can also become her downfall.

How was this spiritual veneer so deceptive? The woman was attracted to the tree because of its promise for fulfillment. It offered comfort, connection, and competence. As the woman looked upon the tree, she saw first that "it was good for food." The fruit provided a delicacy for her table without the work of cultivating and producing it. It titillated her taste buds with the sensational promise of goodness. She became acutely aware of her hunger. How she desired to satisfy the cravings stirring within her! She yearned to experience the comfort this food would bring to her body.

Like Eve, single and married women seek comfort in our distresses. When we feel the sting of rejection, we open the refrigerator door. When we are disillusioned and discouraged, we surf the internet or plug in headphones. When we are overwhelmed with life, we escape into romance novels. When we sob in disappointment, we grab our cell phones and call a friend. We learn quickly what best comforts our hearts, and we become addicted to its taste. In our desire for consolation and relief, we turn to the Tree of Knowledge of Good and Evil and thus ignore the Tree of Life—Jesus!

While standing by the tree and gazing at the fruit, the woman's desire quickened. She connected with its beauty. It promised life. She saw it was "pleasant to the eyes." It looked nothing like death. We may wonder how this woman could have imagined death, never having experienced it. This is where she needed to trust God for what she did not know or understand. What she saw with her eyes only clouded her perspective, dazzling her with the promise of deep connection with God. She longed to be god-like, knowing good and evil, and desire engaged her heart. In her desire for connection with the beauty of this fruit, she succumbed to temptation.

Women today, like Eve, still long for heart connections to satisfy their deepest hunger—the hunger to be loved. They lust for relationships that potentially offer fulfillment, but instead are harmful to their souls. Women who gaze toward forbidden fruit compromise their integrity. The forbidden fruit may be a male peer, friend, employer, pastor, or counselor who is not free to reciprocate an attraction. Any time a woman is tempted by an enticing veneer of inappropriate connection, she must turn away from the forbidden fruit. Women wrongly assume that their hunger for love will be satiated when they are finally connected to a man. True connection can only happen when a woman's spirit is in oneness with the Father's will and purpose.

The woman in the garden saw the tree as providing comfort to her body. Next, she believed it would bring her the beauty of connection, and now she discovered the tree held yet a third promise. It had what it took to make one wise. The fruit could make her competent in what she lacked. She would be god-like, knowing both good and evil. Well, wasn't this necessary in a garden that had potential predators? She would gain greater power to live and survive in this world. Being "wise" would establish her competence, self-worth, and identity.

How loath we women are to be incompetent in our careers, homes, and marriages! We strategize on how we might improve. We voraciously read self-help books. We eagerly attend every seminar and workshop. We work hard to excel. We also begin competing with other women for position and popularity. We are tempted to use our friends as the standard for our success, working hard to surpass them. We seek to be a goddess to whom everyone bows. This requires others to rise to our ideals and expectations.

Deceived by a spiritual veneer, the woman was attracted to the promises of this tree. Comfort, connection, and competence were at her fingertips. Throwing all caution aside, she reached toward the fruit and savored her first bite. Never had she experienced anything like this! She tasted what God had said not to taste. Alas, the opening of her eyes was not a gift, but a tragedy— her innocence was gone, never to be reclaimed.

SHAME DEMANDS A COVERING

For the first time ever, the woman in the Garden of Eden felt vulnerability at a base level. It is true that she acted in disobedience to God, but her unbelief was the greater transgression. She sinned in her unbelief, and innocence was lost. She now stood in the knowledge of her transgression, seeing evil and good for what they were. In sudden awareness that she stood naked before God and her husband, the woman trembled with fear and shame.

Both the woman and man became body-conscious after partaking of the fruit. Can you imagine their shame-stricken eyes when the moment of lustful indulgence passed? What had been veiled in innocence was now uncovered by their knowledge and unbelief. God's command was not intended to withhold, but to preserve. Exposed, stripped of the covering of sinless innocence and selfless love, they beheld their human forms and gender differences in brokenness. They were stricken with guilt and condemnation. In that moment the woman's body and beauty experienced loss and opened her to the vulnerability of external and internal shame. The exposure and self-consciousness struck her heart at a level unknown to her before.

The power of shame in a woman's life is so potent that it generally causes her to attempt one of two things: concealment or defiance. She may cower as weak and pathetic or project herself in shameless brazenness. The emotion of shame is brutal. It will shred any confidence in her femininity. The woman in the garden determined not to feel her deep shame and accompanying fear, so she began taking measures to reduce their lethal power.

She and the man could not endure each other's eyes. Exposure demanded a covering for the shame it produced. In a feeble attempt to cover their vulnerability, they sewed together fig leaves to wear. Then they cowered in a grove of trees for protection. The fig leaves and the grove of trees hid their true selves from each other, but not from God. The pair who had known perfect oneness and completeness shuddered with fear as God's voice came. They were fearful of themselves, fearful of each other, and fearful of a God whom they had disobeyed. No longer did they feel the trust and harmony granted by a union of oneness.

Fear always reduces the possibility to love sacrificially. Adam and his woman now needed to protect their own hearts, which required them to close their hearts to each other. They became gods who would judge good and evil from a limited perspective. This human perspective blinded them to the goodness of God. Each held the possibility of grasping jurisdiction over his life and vying for positional power over the other. Neither could willingly bow in service to the other, lest his own personhood be diminished. Fear intruded as they stood together in the stark nakedness of shame and heard God speak. "'Have you eaten from the tree of which I commanded you that you should not eat?'" (Genesis 3:11).

THE BLAME GAME

Fear and shame produced a strange new communication between the man and woman—blame. When Adam blamed his woman for their shameful condition and transgression, she was caught between a rock and a hard place. For the first time she felt the intense disappointment of not being loved unconditionally. She felt the sting of her husband's justified blame. He said, "'The woman whom You gave to be with me, she gave me of the tree, and I ate'" (Genesis 3:12).

Adam made no mention to God that he saw and heard the serpent deceive the woman. Forget the fact that he stood in the presence of this interchange! Nor did Adam indicate that he chose to compromise. No confession of his willful transgression was forthcoming. Adam's fear and shame became volatile. He hurled his accusation against God. Adam blamed God for giving him a woman who caused him to disobey His command. Shame struggles when exposed, and whenever possible will shift blame to an accomplice. In shame, Eve also joined in the blame game, attempting to justify her actions when she spoke. She was perhaps closer to the truth of what really happened: "'The serpent deceived me, and I ate'" (Genesis 3:13). Her honest admission of wrong meshed with blame. She called attention to the imposter who beguiled her, but not to her husband's presence, or her act of independence from him.

God was not fooled. His knowledge penetrated the grove of trees and the inadequacy of fig leaves. The man and woman's hearts lay exposed under His piercing gaze. What they had done could not be hidden. Though they tried to escape the knowledge of their wrongdoing, justifying one's sin never adequately deflects fear or covers shame.

WOMEN WEARING FIG LEAVES

Shame is intrinsic to humanity. It entered the day the woman was deceived, when she and Adam transgressed. Our eyes bear witness to the shame we feel. As women, we cannot stand the intensity of a gaze that penetrates into the depths of our souls. We drop our eyes lest another see our insecurity. We turn our heads to escape the knowledge or scorn of others. We cannot bear to feel shame or to be shamed. We long for a covering to repel the searching eyes of others. Whether single or married, women sew together their own fig leaves in an attempt to hide from God and each other. We go to great measures to find fig leaves adequate to hide our bodies, our relationships, and our desires.

BODY SHAME

What is seen as more intrinsic to a woman's femininity than her body? Whether she is married or single, she is conscious of her body's form, shape, size, and color.

A woman feels shame when she realizes that her body is imperfect. Either she is too heavy or too skinny. She is too tall, or her face too plain. She begins hating her body and becomes caught in the serpent's snare. He delights in implanting the lies that she is not worthy of love, that she is not beautiful, that she is not competent. A single woman is tempted to measure her worth by the amount of male attention she receives. Her suppositions affirm that her body's imperfection is the basic cause for a lack of attention and acceptance by men. The married woman's self-worth is often determined by her husband's acceptance or rejection of her body's flaws and limitations.

Women who focus on their bodily imperfections design their own fig leaves, as did the woman in the garden. Shame can drive women to food addictions of dieting or binging. Other times women take extreme methods to beautify what they see as a gross bodily flaw. Some use excessive make-up. Some wear shapeless clothing to cover the shame they feel. Others incite attention with seductive clothing. Some swathe their shame with negative, self-devaluing, derogatory words. Women do everything possible to make their fig leaves adequate so they do not need to stand in the shame of their body's imperfections.

RELATIONAL SHAME

Can you imagine the shame that washed over Eve when she realized she had failed her husband? We do not know what her first thoughts were, but perhaps as they sewed the fig leaves, Adam blamed her for the situation. She could see the accusation in his eyes, and she heard it in his voice. How could she get past the shame of her failure in this relationship? The only hope she held was the promise that a Redeemer would break the power of the serpent's lies (See Genesis 3:14-15).

The greatest key to a woman's heart is someone's commitment to her at an intimate level. How she longs to be accepted and loved, by both women and men! She assumes others' level of acceptance either affirms or disqualifies her as a woman worthy of love. To fail her friends is to fail herself. And she is equally devastated when relationships fail her. In such moments her eyes cloud with shame, for the cords of friendships are inherently bound to her selfhood and her heart. Unable to prove her worthiness, she once again walks to her wardrobe, pulls out her fig leaves, and hides from her relationships.

So deeply rooted is our shame that we fear to be truly known. It is far easier to don our relational masks than to allow others to see our inadequacies. We hide relationally from people in two ways. Either we become passive or we become aggressive.

When passive, we work at being nice women and good Christians. We never explode in anger; we never cry in disappointment; we never feel anything too deeply. We falsely believe no one can shame us if we do the right things and say the right things. Such platonic passivity is not life-giving.

When we choose aggressive avenues, we lash out with strong, angry words. We intimidate by our scathing looks and scornful attitudes. We take a volatile, powerful approach in our effort to cover our own shame by shaming others.

Both the passive and aggressive modes conceal the subtle determination that we must never be shamed or in need of the redemption of Jesus. We manage and manipulate instead of turning to the Healer of Hearts. The truth is that we do fail in relationships—we are human and need redemption.

SHAME OF DESIRE

We have discussed the effects of shame in the physical and relational realms. Now let's think about how shame might interface with our desires. The woman in the garden halted long enough at the tree to experience the rise of desire. She longed to have the thing that was withheld from her. She wrapped herself in a desire that superseded God's command. Desire becomes a far more powerful force when it fixates on the promise of life and personal happiness. Eve's desire had spiritual and generational implications.

It is important to realize that desires are the wellspring of motivation. They enable us to make life choices as God's image bearers. However, desires do reveal the truth about our hearts, for our desires are driven by our intrinsic motivations. What we want is shaped by who we are.

Some single women feel guilty that they desire marriage. Why? Usually two reasons surface. We may assume that it is God's will for us to be single, since He brought no man into our lives. Far be it from us to rebel against the will of God! We will more easily reference His eternal plan for our marital status than feel the shame of exposing our desire for marriage. The second skewed assumption is that it is wrong to desire something we do not have. Should we not just accept our lot in life? Did Paul not say, "Now godliness with contentment is great gain"? (1 Timothy 6:6). Yes, indeed he did! Contentment, however, does not squelch desire; it has everything to do with desire. Contentment acknowledges that the heat of desire is present, but willingly surrenders that desire to the purposes and timing of God.

Marriage is not superseding God's command. Rather it is one of His commandments. Remember, Jesus referred to this imperative that was spoken in the beginning, "'For this reason a man shall leave his father and mother and be joined to his wife, and the two shall become one flesh'" (Matthew 19:5). The Proverbs writer suggested there is such a strong desire for marriage that a man will go in search of it. He said, "He who finds a wife finds a good thing, and obtains favor from the LORD" (Proverbs 18:22). Desiring marriage is good and proper; it is when we distrust God for our marital status that we act in unbelief. When we take matters into our hands, we limit God's work in our lives. It is not for us to construct, produce, or eradicate our desires. This route leads inevitably to shame. But how then do we live?

ANOTHER WAY

Do you remember the story of my attraction to a man at the beginning of the chapter? Was my sin demanding that this man should be the fulfillment of a deep desire to be loved? Did I hold to the belief that he alone would offer life in ways I had not yet experienced? Had I opened my heart to a god other than the Lord God? Did I feel shame because I had tasted the forbidden fruit? These are questions we as women must ask ourselves. In those moments of longing, God beckons us to turn our faces toward Him. He wants His daughters to "desire much, pray for much, but demand nothing. To trust God means to demand nothing."[3]

Life is not found in getting or having the perfect Christian husband. Life is not found in beauty or popularity. Life is not found in comfort, connection, or competence. No, fullness of life is found in turning ourselves toward the scrutiny and gaze of a Redeemer whose eyes are full of love and mercy. Life is in opening our hearts to the Lover of our souls who walks with us in all of our relationships. And finally, life is turning our spirits toward the Tree of Life, who fills all our desires with His wholeness. Thus, our shameful fig leaves will be exchanged for a robe of God's righteousness, and we will bask in the glory of His freedom and truth forever!

chapter six

EMBRACING FEMININITY

One wintry day in the land of Narnia, Edmund met the powerful White Witch. She tempted Edmund aboard her royal sledge by craftily offering him Turkish delight. Enamored by her generosity, Edmund joined her and ate the delectable treat to his heart's content. Before the White Witch released Edmund, she demanded that his siblings join him next time if he wanted more Turkish delight. Upon returning home, Edmund realized that he must keep this adventure a secret, for his siblings believed the White Witch was Narnia's foe.

Some days later the four siblings unexpectedly entered Narnia together and were guided to Mr. and Mrs. Beaver's house. Edmund didn't enjoy his meal very much in the Beavers' home because his mouth salivated for the delectable Turkish delight he had eaten before in Narnia. At an opportune time, he quietly left the Beavers' home in search of the White Witch's palace and her Turkish delight.

After trudging through the snow for a long time, Edmund finally arrived at the palace door. To his surprise, he met the doorkeeper, a fierce wolf. After conferring with the witch, the wolf allowed Edmund entrance to see her. The White Witch was in a surly mood and became quite angry that Edmund had not brought along his siblings. He hesitantly requested some Turkish delight, but he was instantly silenced. In a few short moments, things went from bad to worse in the wake of the White Witch's wrath as she declared war against Aslan the great lion, his loyalists, and Edmund's siblings.

Edmund soon realized on that awful night that he had too much loved a forbidden thing. His secret love of Turkish delight could adversely affect the destiny of his siblings and the land of Narnia forever.

Like Edmund, daughters of Eve are also tempted with secret loves. Succumbing to the allure of forbidden fruit ultimately brings shame and consequences, just as it did for the first woman in the garden. Eve's consequences affected her in the areas of greatest vulnerability: her femininity and sexuality. "To the woman [God] said: 'I will greatly multiply your sorrow and your conception; in pain you shall bring forth children; your desire shall be for your husband, and he shall rule over you'" (Genesis 3:16). The consequence was twofold. She would experience physical suffering in childbirth, and she would struggle relationally in the union of oneness. What consequence could be more devastating? For a woman's identity is intrinsically wrapped in her ability to bear children and her beauty of femininity.[†]

[†] An unmarried woman is most fulfilled when she can offer her gift of assistance to her church or community through her profession, in coming alongside as a "help meet" in the broader sense.

THE MYSTERY OF FEMININITY IN THE AFFECTIVE DOMAIN

The mystery of a woman's sexual capacity is God-given. Her femininity is an expression of His creativity and is designed to give her identity and completeness. She alone holds the power to retain its mystery with gracious honor or to exploit it with careless abandon. How does a virtuous single woman fully embrace and protect the mystery, beauty, and glory of her womanhood?

A single woman may question whether she can truly be a whole person without experiencing all aspects of her sexuality. A woman's sexuality is more than the physical ability to participate in the act of marriage, to grow a child in her womb, and to give sustenance to her young. In her essay "Singleness and Sexuality," Martha Good Smith said,

> *Too often sexuality has been seen only within the context of marriage, an idea which has dominated our attitudes in the past. When all persons are accepted as sexual beings, however, persons outside of a marriage relationship can be included with ease in male and female fellowship as sexual beings created in the image of God.*[1]

Femininity and masculinity are gifts meant to glorify God and honor each other.

The mystery of sexuality permits definitive expressions of the "instincts, drives, and behavior"[2] unique to males and females. All women embracing their sexuality need to understand their embedded instincts of mothering and nurturing, their drive for emotional intimacy, and their innate responses to pain and joy. These aspects of femininity are imparted by God in making us distinctly *women*, whether we are single or married.

MOTHERING AND NURTURING

Young girls do not need to be taught how to hold and cuddle a baby. Cradling is instinctive to a female because she is called to participate in God's work by having babies. Her strong maternal instincts heighten as she grows into adulthood. Often a young bride will begin thinking of a baby soon after the excitement of her wedding day has dissipated and her marriage has taken on a measure of routine. She is obsessed with one thought. She wants a baby. So strong is the desire for nurturing and mothering that at times she will go to extreme measures to have and hold a child of her own.

Recall the story in Scripture of two women who each gave birth to a baby. When one infant died, each mother argued that the live baby was her own. They went to King Solomon to settle the dispute. When he answered that they should cut the child in half so that each could have a part, the birth mother was horrified. For the sake of her child's life, she would willingly give him to the other woman. She passed the test as the birth mother and got her baby back.

Even today, women will use extreme methods to have children. They will spend thousands of dollars to adopt a child or to pay a surrogate mother. In 2008, *Time Magazine* carried a heart-wrenching article about a group of high school girls who had made a pact to get pregnant and raise their children together.[3] Many of the babies conceived by the seventeen unwed mothers had the same father. The ladies of the pact who got negative pregnancy test results were more disappointed than relieved. While we may be shocked that these teens felt no shame in their immoral lifestyle, their story bears witness to women's strong desire to mother and nurture.

Every grown, healthy woman has daily and monthly reminders of her body's potential. Other women also mirror to her what the female body is capable of producing and nurturing. No matter where she turns, she cannot escape this knowledge of her sexuality. In fact, she is never more woman than when she is with child. Barbara Feil, a part-time professor at Multnomah Bible College, once said, "My own childlessness has made me very aware that not all women are mothers, but I've always considered the most profound scriptural truth about the roles of men and women to be that women have the babies."[4]

My friend Lois, who is a nurse, said this to single ladies: "We women are active participators in God's creation when we embrace our cycles and our ability to bear children." She was not saying that single women should violate their purity for the sake of having a baby. Rather she called us to agree with God's purposes and design for womanhood. She encouraged the single women to accept with gratitude their bodies' capabilities and their longing to nurture as mothers.

EMOTIONAL INTIMACY

A second aspect of a woman's sexuality is her intense desire for emotional intimacy with a male. Emotional connection validates her need for belonging and security. For women, emotional connection is fostered through conversation and kindness. When a man patiently listens to her expressed feelings and responds with kind words, she is quickly charmed and drawn to him.

She anticipates that marriage is the key to fulfillment of her need for emotional intimacy. Often her expectations are severely tested after marriage, when she begins to feel that her body may be more important to her husband than her heart. Her demands for emotional intimacy in marriage produce instead a bitter struggle of the wills.

Single women may be unaware that a man's emotional needs are often met through physical intimacy. Initially, a man may draw a woman to himself through emotional intimacy. A single woman is in a precarious position when she allows emotional intimacy with a man who has not made his intentions known to her. He has engaged her heart without a commitment to her.

How then can a woman's need for emotional intimacy be met outside of marriage? Her connection with men in general cannot provide a substitute for the intimacy of marriage. Neither can she capture a surrogate satisfaction from other relational sources, and live with every desire met. Intimate connection with a man is reserved for within a committed relationship. But remember, marriage does not fill every hunger either. Only God is enough. There are many times when we as women must offer our unfulfilled longings to Him, allowing His love and comfort to satisfy us in a way no human relationship can.

Meaningful, appropriate male and female relationships do exist outside the marriage covenant. When we learn to draw our belonging and security from relationship with God, we are freed to share in a wider spectrum of male and female completion. In God's economy, femininity and masculinity offer to each other unique and precious gifts that cannot be received from any other source.

Later in Martha Good Smith's essay, she writes,

> The most basic [relationship] consists of a male-
> female fellowship expressing itself in a variety
> of relationships, each of which is beneficial both
> to the individual and to the society as a whole.
> A group of persons composed of married and
> single men and women that is committed to meet
> regularly for discussion, fellowship, caring, and
> sharing provides a climate in which a variety of
> relationships may exist. Within this context the
> individual gives and receives, nourishes, and is
> nourished. Thus the person's contact with the larger
> society has a quality of depth that reflects mature
> awareness and appreciation of self and others...
> Within this framework human sexuality moves far
> beyond the desire for physical expression.[5]

The single life must not become an isolated life. Though
alone in one sense, we find ourselves a part of a Christian community filled with godly men and women. In a broader sense,
we belong to the people of God and find with them a wealth of
friendship and connection. We can experience harmony, validation, and joy as we honor each other in meaningful and appropriate relationships.

TEARS AND LAUGHTER

A third facet of a woman's femininity in the affective domain
is her innate ability to respond to life's joy and pain. She laughs
quickly when she is happy and free. She cries easily when she is
stricken with hurt and sorrow.

Why did the woman receive the consequence of sorrow for eating the fruit? The woman's consequences were fundamentally different from Adam's. His thorns and thistles affronted the productivity of his masculinity, but her pain and sorrow affronted the vulnerability of her femininity. She would bring forth children with pain, and she would have an intense longing for emotional intimacy. Her pain, disappointment, and joy in these two areas would find expression primarily through her tears and laughter.

A woman is often shamed by her tears. She loathes having others see her disappointment, pain, and sorrow. In her shame, she formulates vows to hide her weakness. If a woman refuses to embrace her tears, she becomes unfeeling and harsh. There is a distinction here: manipulative tears are hurtful and selfish when they are used to control circumstances or relationships. Godly tears are an acknowledgement that life is beyond a woman's ability to control and that she needs God to intervene. Not always is it appropriate to let others see her tears, but she must feel them in her heart and offer them as a gift to God. She is called to embrace the kind of tears that later will water her season of joy.

A woman who can bring her tears to God can also bring her laughter. A woman's laughter sets everything right in her home and world. The old adage bears out the truth of this idea: "If mamma ain't happy, ain't nobody happy." A woman's positive and negative emotions do affect her home and her workplace. Laughter is born out of two things. The woman who laughs freely is at peace: with herself, with others, and with God. Second, laughter is the fruit of gratefulness. A grateful woman has relinquished the demand that life revolve around her. A woman's capacity for laughter empowers her to live with abandon and bring refreshment to a world full of disappointment. Our tears and laughter are both innately feminine qualities. They are windows revealing inner strength, and a heart engaged with life. Paula Rinehart says:

> *The strength of vulnerability is a curious mixture of discovering your heart and sharing your real self, as best you can, with the people God has put in your life. You can't shut down on the inside without quelling the very passion that makes the journey worthwhile. Those walls around the heart take buckets of energy to maintain and God has better things for his children to do. When we close off our hearts, we dishonor him.*[6]

Honestly bringing her tears and laughter before God and others makes a woman femininely soft, inviting, and alive.

THE MYSTERY OF FEMININITY IN THE PHYSICAL DOMAIN

God designed and created the physical bodies of men and women. They are distinctly male and female. In His infinite wisdom, He placed in these bodies hormone levels that would induce desire, creating in each a need for the other. These desires are not wrong; nor are they unspiritual. Quite the opposite!

Both younger and older virtuous single women have been frustrated with their strong desires for marriage and intimacy, feeling the tension of godly boundaries. How does one remain pure in the throes of desire? We must recognize that the physical and emotional realms make us most acutely aware of desire. Our bodies and souls have needs and cravings. They stir up desires when they become aware of a perceived lack. They crave the comfort of fulfillment. When our bodies are exhausted, we long for sleep. When they are hungry, we desire food. When our hearts are lonely, we yearn for companionship. Desire seeks fullness.

Certainly being a Christian does not eradicate desire. I would suggest that the more alive a woman is in Christ, the more alive will she be in all aspects of her feminine desires. Shannon Ethridge fleshes out this idea with the imagery of a table and its four legs in her book, *Every Woman's Battle*. The tabletop has the title: "A Life of Balance and Integrity." Each table leg is one of the four components in the make-up of a human being. She lists the four as spiritual, emotional, physical, and mental. Then she says,

> By definition, our sexuality isn't **what we do**. Even people who are committed to celibacy are sexual beings. Our sexuality is **who we are**, and we are made with body, mind, heart, and spirit, not just a body. Therefore, sexual integrity is not just about physical chastity. It is about purity in all four aspects of our being (body, mind, heart, and spirit). When all four aspects line up perfectly, our "tabletop" (our life) reflects balance and integrity.[7]

When we as women embrace our desires for love and marriage, we are agreeing with God's purpose for mankind. Our tendency is to resist embracing all aspects of our womanhood, for this also means embracing the possibility of disappointment. We find that "the most common way to handle desire is to find a way to deaden it, to pretend it doesn't exist. We reduce desire to a level we can manage and control."[8]

In our vice of managing and controlling our desires, we are tempted to compare our lives with others. We measure our lack of fulfillment by others' fullness. This makes us question God's goodness. We must understand that not all is equal in a fallen world. There are godly women who do experience the fulfillment of financial security, meaningful friendships, a devout husband, and marital intimacy. To the casual observer, it may seem that some Christian people have it made. Others are out of luck.

Evelyn Mumaw, in her book *Woman Alone*, made the observation that some godly people enjoy both the temporal, short-lived pleasures, and the spiritual satisfactions. She indicated this is not the norm, saying,

> *The large majority of Christians…live with unmet needs of one sort or another. For some reason God chooses to permit many Christians to have their need for food unmet. And many others have their need for physical security unfulfilled. It is more typical than atypical for us to live with some unmet needs and hungers.*[9]

If it is true that there are many unmet needs in the world, is it true that single women will have unmet needs and desires? Indeed it is!

How do single women live with unmet needs and desires in their lives? They are tempted to respond with desperation. They demonstrate it in their determination to make life work according to their ideals and comfort zones. They consciously and unconsciously repress their femininity. They exploit their bodies in the search for gratification. Is there any other way for single women to respond to the disappointment of their unmet needs? Could it be that when single women embrace their sexuality, they actually reserve their virginity and feminine mystique? Let us look at these options a bit more closely.

HUNGRY WOMEN WITH UNMET DESIRES

For many years, my parents were actively involved with a city mission in Elkhart, Indiana. Most times they took us children along in their ministry to the street people. As an impressionable young child, I never quite knew what to think of men who had no homes or families. As the city mission grew, it opened its doors to women as well. These broken women did not fit into any of my prior categories. Some looked despondent, others hardened.

One evening we had been at the city mission, and were driving home through a darkened part of town. To my amazement I saw several houses with red lights. "Look!" I exclaimed, "Those houses have red lights!"

My mother did not miss a beat and said, "Those houses have women who do things that are not good. They turn that light on to let men know they are there."

At the time her answer was sufficient for an innocent young girl. It wasn't until I was older that I really understood the implications of a red light zone, and the brokenness surrounding it.

As an adult many years later, I found myself waiting to pull into a busy intersection. Suddenly a large, red blinking light across the street caught my eye. How my heart sank! Someone was offering a twisted love in a hotel room, when in reality she desired pure love. Today the absolutes of right and wrong are muddled in our Western world. Women feel free to do whatever their drives and instincts dictate. While many teenage girls and single women do not consider themselves promiscuous, they still engage in immoral lifestyles. In the new "hook-up generation," they see their sexual activities as a normal part of male and female friendships.

Many of these single women are unaware of how deeply immorality damages their souls through the mysterious power of intimate connection. "The mystery of bonding in sex is an inviolate one; sex creates a bond whether we want one or not. That's why shame, betrayal, and loss are hard to shake when a woman has slept with a man and the relationship dissolves."[10]

Why do women give and sell their bodies to men—or to other women—who care nothing for their hearts but only for personal satisfaction? Far too often, Christian women have a tendency to secretly scorn immoral women. Rarely are kind words spoken or compassion shown to women who blatantly stand on street corners, flash red lights, or participate in lesbian activities. There is something repulsive about these lifestyles, yet we are called to minister to such people. Jesus did.

Before we judge others too harshly from our limited perspective, let's look at a few possible root causes for why a woman may not retain her virginity. I suggest three: she may be involved in an immoral lifestyle because she is a victim of circumstance, because she is emotionally estranged from her father, or because she has compromised moral standards in her desire for belonging and acceptance.

VICTIMS OF CIRCUMSTANCE

One summer during my graduate studies, I took a course on *Education and Social Issues*. My professor, Dr. Marcia Sheridan, shared with the class a tragic documentary video of brothel houses in the larger cities of Ethiopia. Many families in rural villages face survival challenges with their lack of food and money. To keep from starving, they send their young daughters (ten years or older—sometimes younger) to the brothel houses. The girls are clothed and fed for their services rendered, and their families are compensated. In the documentary's testimonials, these young ladies dreamed of the day they would marry someone rich who would help them escape. They did not reside there out of their own volition, but were imprisoned by physical needs. My heart cried out for these lovely young girls who hated what they did, but found it their lifeline for survival.

I once read an article in a local newspaper about a single mom who worked at a strip joint. She hated the job, but saw it as a means to an end. Lucrative jobs were scarce in her hometown area. In the meantime, she was going to school, desiring to improve her quality of life. She hoped her degree would enable her to find a better job and walk away from the place that violated her womanhood. Unfortunately, this woman used her body to provide for herself and her child because she knew no other options.

These are only two examples of women who find themselves in helpless circumstances. Their physical needs ultimately drive them to compromise their virginity and fidelity. The profundity of such damage is the loss of innocence and feminine vulnerability. A woman has become an object to be possessed instead of a person to be valued and treasured as God's image bearer.

LACKING EMOTIONAL CONNECTEDNESS

A woman has an intense need for emotional connectedness with her father, from girlhood into adulthood. If she has a father who is emotionally or physically absent, she may try to find connection elsewhere, often in unhealthy ways. The absence of a strong, loving father often drives her to blindly seek closeness with other men or women.[†] When she first experiences intimate but illegitimate connection with another person, she finds only a pseudo-connection. In her internal emptiness, she is driven to go back again and again, compromising her body in her hunger for connectedness.

If this woman should marry, two things will surface. It is likely that she will seek a spouse who can create the father image she never had. She will be tempted to relate to him as a daughter instead of a team player and a wife. Secondly, whenever she has been physically and sexually intimate with a person outside the boundaries of marital oneness, she has created soul bonds and ties. In order for the marriage to survive and flourish, these ties need to be broken.

[†] If a father violates his daughter's body, he transgresses against her very soul and damages her severely. Only the redemption and mercy of Jesus can heal her multi-faceted emotional wounds.

A daughter's close relationship with her mother, and with God the Father, will provide a powerful safeguard against reacting to her father by pursuing ungodly relationships.

SEEKING ACCEPTANCE

As adult women, we become accountable for our life choices. Our choices reflect everything that has shaped our lives. Sometimes we compromise with our choices. Women who have grown up in dysfunctional homes often have few boundaries, if any. In their hunger for acceptance, belonging, and love, they are tempted to compromise areas of their virginity.

Compromising is a dangerous thing. The Proverbs writer warned us of what happens when we engage in activities outside of God's boundaries. "Can a man take fire to his bosom, and his clothes not be burned? Can one walk on hot coals, and his feet not be seared?" (6:27-28).

Is there hope for heart-hungry women with unmet needs? The answer is a resounding "Yes!" Our hope is defined and embodied in the Person of Jesus Christ. Our hope is attached to His fullness of grace and mercy with resources unlimited. Because of Him, it is possible for every single woman to retain her virginity and every married woman to live with uncompromising fidelity. How is this done? Let's begin by defining virginity.

VIRGINITY DEFINED

"I don't know what to do! How could he do this to me?" Carol cried out despairingly.

My heart ached for my friend. Carol's fiancé had just called off their engagement, and it seemed that all her dreams for love and happiness were shredded in one short moment.

Throwing her hands to her face, she moaned softly, "What will people do when they find out? I think I will lose my mind." I attempted to comfort her. "People will understand. They will know that it was not you that broke this engagement." "Oh, but I don't know what to do. What will people say?" she insisted.

Our conversation circled around the shame Carol felt about her broken marriage engagement. I left that evening feeling confused, but also sorrowing for my friend's loss. However, there was more to the story that I did not know that evening. Carol was deathly afraid of a known truth within herself, one she could not bring herself to expose.

Some weeks later I discovered that my friend Carol was pregnant. Suddenly I understood the context of our discussion that warm summer evening three months earlier. My friend's fiancé had stolen Carol's virginity and then walked out of her life. Now Carol was left to pick up the shattered pieces. Only God in His mercy could redeem what was taken from her.

Maybe you have read the last few sections of this chapter thinking, "This really does not apply to me." It may be true that you are not a woman in the depths of depravity. You are not living an immoral lifestyle. You have not compromised your virginity. You may even have lived a very strict self-controlled life. However, is that the sum total of virginity? Is virginity only abstinence from something, or is there more? The Apostle Paul's definition of a virgin was not about abstaining from something, but about embracing something. He said, "There is a difference between a wife and a virgin. The unmarried woman cares about the things of the Lord, *that she may be holy both in body and in spirit*" (I Corinthians 7:34, emphasis added). What does it mean to be holy both in body and in spirit?

HOLY IN BODY

Beth curled on the chair, shifted nervously, and said, "Thank you for allowing me to come and talk with you." Her eyes downcast, she added quietly, "I have a continual struggle with something, and I need to share it with someone."

Her words trailed off into a heavy silence. I waited quietly as she pulled on a loose strand of hair and studied the floor, biting her lip.

"Don't be afraid. I won't think any less of you," I encouraged her kindly.

Suddenly she began to talk, spilling out the frustration of her struggle with impure sexual thoughts and habits. She hated how they controlled her, but she felt helpless to change. "I feel so ashamed and guilty. I want to change. Can you help me?" she asked imploringly.

Christian single women, like Beth, long to be pure, chaste women who are above reproach. Time and time again, godly women vow that they will break their sexually impure activities and habits, but in moments of weakness, they succumb to temptation. Afterward they wallow in shame and disillusionment. They berate themselves for their lack of self-control. They are tempted to hate their sexuality. They cannot embrace the beauty and mystery of who God created them to be. Being holy in body seems like an impossible feat.

How does a single woman attain the level of holiness Paul

instructed for a virgin? First, we need to remind ourselves that the desire for intimacy is a God-given desire. It does not appear out of a vacuum; neither is it self-induced. God created us with physical and sexual desires and urges, but what we do with them does matter! Paul didn't give a list of things that single women can't do with their bodies, or we would be bound by a law of do's and don'ts. Instead, he invited us as single women to seek a liberating standard of holiness in body. Holiness will result not when we place our focus on *what **not** to do*, but rather when we focus on *who we are in Christ*. Our bodies belong to Him.

Perhaps you are still protesting, "Why should I be excluded from something God has created my body to experience?" God is not attempting to make your life miserable by withholding something from your body. However, He does want to protect the gift a single woman holds within herself—the costly and precious gift of virginity. If virginity is a gift, why is an unmarried woman tempted to compromise it? Often our focus is skewed in dealing with temptation. Let's think about three areas in which we are called to be "holy in body." We will look at holiness in sensory awareness, in the longing for emotional intimacy, and in life disappointments.

Sensory Awareness

Our twenty-first-century lifestyle bombards us daily with all kinds of images that evoke titillating sensations. Has there ever been a more accessible, visually-stimulating culture in history than that found on the American soil of this century? The Tree of Knowledge of Good and Evil still dangles its fruit before our very eyes. Reaching for the fruit is our first step in compromising our loyalty to the One who offers us life instead. Our eyes are entrance gates into the path of evil or the path of life.

We need to make a conscious choice to turn our eyes away from the forbidden tree that dangles unwholesome literature, movies, and websites to incite impure thoughts and habits. Instead, we need to turn our gaze toward "whatever things are true, whatever things are noble, whatever things are just, whatever things are pure, whatever things are lovely, whatever things are of good report" (Philippians 4:8). These things free us to be holy in body and experience the pleasures found in belonging to Christ.

Longing for Emotional Intimacy

One of a woman's most basic needs is for emotional bonding and intimacy. A woman's hunger for connection is like a funneled chalice which needs continual assurance of a committed love. If her funneled chalice runs empty, she will deeply desire to give expression to her need for emotional bonding and intimacy. In her emptiness, she is tempted to fill her need in the context of herself. She may succumb to masturbation, producing sensations that make her feel fully alive and beautiful as a woman. Strangely, she ends up feeling empty and shameful afterward.

Again, the focus dare not be on what she can't do, but on who she is in Christ. In Christ, she finds freedom by forgiving and releasing key people who should have connected with her need for emotional bonding, but did not. In Christ, she is willing not only to forgive and release, but also to pour the goodness of Christ into the lives of those who withheld from her. She is liberated from her addiction to self-connectedness, which then frees her to live in the fulfillment of connectedness to the Lord God, with whom she is one.

Life Disappointments

Disappointed hope bashes its brutal cudgel again and again against the hearts of women. An older single woman is especially susceptible to its damage. When she is disappointed too often, she can easily become hardened. In her hardening, she becomes angry with life, angry with people, and angry with God. Anger in a Christian woman is not always easily detected. Oh, she may dress modestly, smile sweetly, and say the right things, but she hates herself and who she is as a woman. Being holy in one's body is not just an outward performance of holy actions and words. It also rests in the thoughts and motives a woman harbors in the secret rooms of her heart.

Her anger toward disappointing situations and toward God (who could have changed her situation, but did not!) may open the door to sexually impure habits. She becomes angry that God withholds something she desires to have.

Isaiah, one of Israel's prophets, rebuked his people for faulting God's actions. He said, "Woe unto him that striveth with his Maker! Let the potsherd strive with the potsherds of the earth. Shall the clay say to him that fashioneth it, 'What makest thou?' or thy work, 'He hath no hands'?" (Isaiah 45:9 KJV).

I can imagine Isaiah might say to single women today, "God is a holy God. Let God be God. If He chooses to withhold marriage from you, who are you to demand otherwise? If He gives to you the gift of virginity longer than He does others, that is His privilege. Why are you resisting?"

God calls single women to live in the submission of deferred
hope. He wants us to know He sees what we cannot see. In submission to Him we find rest and freedom. When our hearts are
at rest, we are freed from the need to engage in compulsory,
impure habits.

In the Hour of Temptation

We compromise personal purity when we believe lies about
God's truth. In the moment of temptation ask yourself, "What
is it that I really want from this experience?" Answer it honestly.
Next, ask Jesus, the Second Adam, to join you in eating the forbidden fruit. You say, "How ridiculous!" Of course it is!

However, you can cry out to Jesus by asking Him to enter
your moment of temptation. In His humanity, He experienced
every kind of desire and temptation you face, and He is able to
identify with your struggle in the moment (Hebrews 4:15-16).
Turning your face toward Him will open the door for His Spirit
to come alongside, empowering you to resist temptation. Your
path to holiness in body lies in choosing to turn away from the
forbidden fruit, and turn instead to the Tree of Life.

HOLY IN SPIRIT

Why did Paul specifically teach that a virgin should be holy
not only in body but also in spirit? Outward holiness is never
enough. Our physical bodies function according to commands
and within boundaries, but external actions can never produce
holiness. They can only produce an appearance of holiness. We
are more than body; we also have an inner spirit.

The spirit within us is the being that comes from God and goes to God. When we turn toward God, He implants His life within our spirits. We then are redeemed, although there are areas in our soul that still need ongoing sanctification. His life in our spirit now enables us to function with the freedom of His grace.

It is God who empowers us to be holy in body and spirit. The Apostle Peter also understood this. He instructed the early believers, "Just as he who called you is holy, so be holy in all you do; for it is written: 'Be holy, because I am holy'" (I Peter 1:15-16 NIV). Holiness is possible because (and only because) we are born in the righteousness of Jesus Christ.

Men and women are often unaware that when they bring themselves to each other physically or sexually, they also bring their spirits. Human tendency is to judge the sum total of the person in the physical realm. Usually what we receive or do not receive from each other is communicated at a spirit level. Many times our spirits are communicating with each other even when we are not consciously aware of it or audibly verbalizing our thoughts. That is why sometimes people can "feel" the presence of others before they see them.

We first compromise the holiness of the Lord Jesus in our spirits, before we ever compromise in our bodies. There are two primary ways that women compromise in their spirits: through fantasies, and through emotional bonds and ties. A single woman may outwardly conform to the standard of holiness for her body. She does not, however, put a limit on the pseudo-relationships she forms in her spirit. She may rightly judge that a promiscuous lifestyle is overt rebellion against God's call to be "holy in body." However, a woman's unholy fantasies can be covert rebellion against God's call to be "holy in spirit." She is very capable of walking into the red light zone of her mind.

COMPROMISING WITH FANTASIES

Every woman I know is capable of evoking a "phantom man"— the man who will love her perfectly. He might be a man who has the right physique, the right color of eyes, and the right voice. However, most women do not necessarily see his physical aspects as the most critical characteristics of this phantom man; what she does fantasize about is his extreme tenderness and kindness. She imagines him to be a man who whispers his love and connects deeply with her at the emotional level. Dr. Toni Grant used the term *Ghostly Lover* to describe the phantom man.

> The Ghostly Lover can most simply be seen as the great him, the perfect man, Mr. Right, Mr. Wonderful, that man—real or imaginary—that a woman can never have, the Prince Charming that is sure to arrive—someday—on her doorstep, glass slipper in hand. The Ghostly Lover may be a real man, a man she has loved and lost, a love that can never be, or he may be an ideal, a figment of the woman's imagination.
>
> ...It is as if the woman takes the male within herself...idealizes him, and projects that ideal out onto every man she meets. In a very real sense, the Ghostly Lover is the personification of the woman's tendency toward grandiosity...Needless to say, real men cannot meet this test; almost all men fare poorly when compared with a woman's Ghostly Lover.[11]

While I do not agree with Dr. Grant's basic approach to womanhood, her succinct imagery captures the woman's ability to create in her mind what she cannot produce outside of herself. Undoubtedly, this is why a woman is drawn to romance novels and movies. She can passively simulate the perfect romance without being accountable to a human relationship. The subtle messages a woman drinks in through this kind of media cause her to form expectations in her heart, whether she is aware of it or not. Her accumulation of dreamy ideals makes it far more difficult for her to enter the reality of a male and female relationship. I especially caution older single ladies who make this their regular recreational reading diet. They are allowing their hearts to create perfectionist expectations of men. Such fantasies do not crumble easily without the reality of life with a human man.

Fantasies in and of themselves are not necessarily wrong when they are creative imagination. The danger in fantasies is twofold: fantasies can feed desires that are not lawfully satisfied, and fantasies can easily put us of out of touch with reality. Fantasies have the power to create unrealistic expectations of others. Therefore all women, single or married, are tempted to choose or create a phantom man and use him to fantasize the perfect love relationship. These imaginations, ideals, and expectations create an idol we can worship and trust. We then are tempted to measure our real-life man, and any other men, by this idol we have conjured up. We become ungrateful and critical. We begin demanding a standard of ideals instead of receiving the gifts our men have to offer. We begin loving the phantom more than the real. This is engaging in spiritual adultery.

Jesus reminded his disciples that adultery is more than the

act itself; it begins as a motive of the heart. Jesus did not mince words in this teaching. When single and married women begin indulging with a phantom man, they are lusting for something that is forbidden. A woman turning her empty heart to the tender-hearted phantom grieves the Lover of her Soul. Her male relationships will also be adversely affected, because a man's confidence is built by a woman's trust in him and respect for his leadership.

COMPROMISING WITH EMOTIONAL BONDS

A woman enters relationships based on her ability to make heart connections. She has no other way to enter the door of relationships except through emotional bonding. She walks into friendships and away from them *feeling* things. How can this be? Imagine a woman having many coiled cords dangling from her heart. At the end of each coiled cord is a suction cup that attaches to the people she chooses to love. Her heart beats the very life of who she is through these cords. This enables her to be a nurturer in relationships. When she loses a relationship, her cords are torn because of the emotional energy she has given out. That is why her suction cups drop blood and tears when she walks away from a meaningful relationship.

It is not surprising then that any significant friendship with a man ultimately creates a varying level of emotional bonds for a woman. A single woman should use caution in the amount of energy she invests with single males or men not related to her. Her cords should reserve enough elasticity so that the relationships will function at a safe distance, and a healthy giving and receiving will bless both participants.

One can quickly understand the danger of a woman's cords. Her relational cords may attach by mutual agreement, but they may also attach to a perceived relationship. Sometimes a man will tell a woman she is easier to talk to than a man. In this, a man offers his need to her without committing his heart to her. This can create an unhealthy relational bond. The woman compromises her fidelity and attaches to the man in hopes that their relationship will deepen. She then orders and plans her life around this relationship fostering co-dependency.

A co-dependent relationship allows the coiled cord to become taut. At this point, the single woman has inappropriately bonded to the man. My married friend Marie has said of single women, "A woman who becomes emotionally dependent on a man no longer needs to live a life of trusting in God—she is 'risk-free.'" She becomes captive to the man who determines her decisions. She relinquishes personal responsibility for her choices.

Emotional bonding is right and good if it is in the context of a committed, pure relationship. Far too often for single ladies it is not. If the relationship is not a lifelong commitment, it is imperative that a woman break free from unhealthy emotional bonding. Inappropriate bonding or intimate thoughts from previous interactions also will greatly affect a woman's future relationships, if these connections are not broken. She has given parts of her heart away through emotional bonding.[†]

A woman who chooses to be holy in spirit will not put

[†] The forming and breaking of soul bonds will be discussed in more detail in Chapter 10.

herself, or her present or future marriage, in jeopardy for the sake of her need for fulfillment. She will hold her friendships with reverence and guarded respect.

THE MYSTERY REVEALED

An unmarried woman who is holy in her body and holy in her spirit has turned her focus toward God. She recognizes that God is not withholding something precious and good, but is graciously protecting the mystery of her virginity and fidelity. The sacred joining of a man and wife is, in part, a picture of what God intends for the consummation of all things in Jesus and His bride, the church. What is now withheld from single people will not be withheld in the new heaven and new earth. Single and married people alike will then experience in their redeemed bodies what the union of oneness was only foreshadowing, as they bring their gifts of virginity and fidelity to the marriage supper of the Lamb!

chapter seven

FORSAKEN AND GRIEVED

Hugging her knees to herself, twenty-eight-year-old Cyndi sat under the maple tree watching a robin and its mate hopping along searching for juicy worms. "Even birds find their mates and raise young," she muttered cynically, reflecting on the phone call she had received from her friend Amy the day before.

"Cyndi," Amy had said eagerly, "I have some news! Could I come over to your place to share it with you?"

"Sure thing!" she had replied.

Ten minutes later, a curious Cyndi had greeted her smiling friend at the door and invited her inside. After pouring two glasses of cold lemonade and making small talk, they both headed toward the patio. Cyndi could see that Amy was bursting with excitement. "Okay, what's up?" she asked as they sat down.

"Cyndi, you won't believe it! Someone stopped by my house last evening for a short while. He would like to pursue a friendship with me. Guess who!" Amy said excitedly.

"Amy! I'm so happy for you!" Cyndi said, caught up by her friend's delight. "Do I know him?" she asked.

"Oh, yes! You do know him," Amy smiled, nodding enthusiastically.

Cyndi started guessing, but she was nowhere close to the right answer. "I give up," she finally said laughingly.

Amy dropped her voice. "It was Rob!" Her eyes shone.

Stunned, Cyndi looked at her friend, her thoughts racing furiously. She had long admired Rob, a godly man and dynamic leader. She had harbored the secret hope that someday Rob would initiate a special friendship with her. Caught in a split second's hesitation, she realized her friend still was waiting for a response. She forced a smile.

"Congratulations! I am happy for you," she repeated warmly, swallowing her initial disappointment.

"Are you okay with this?" asked Amy hesitantly. "I wanted you to hear it from me before you hear it from anyone else," she added almost apologetically.

"Yes, I am just surprised," Cyndi replied. "Amy, I have no claims on this man. He has asked you, not me...I want you to be happy with him."

They chatted a while longer, and then Amy left. A myriad of conflicting emotions surged through Cyndi. She was truly happy for her friend, but she also felt profoundly disappointed. She determined not to cry. If Rob did not choose to move toward her, so be it. She would not succumb to her disappointment through tears, and neither would she let this destroy her friendship with Amy. She would be Christian in her attitudes and forget about the sadness of her own heart. Life was more than Rob.

Thousands of disappointed singles identify with Cyndi's story. More than one woman has been bypassed by a man she admired, or has listened to a friend excitedly share about her new courtship. Disappointed women have two options. They can choose to acknowledge their feelings, or choose to ignore them. Women often do not recognize that emotional triggers are an opportunity to open one's heart more fully toward God. "Ignoring our emotions is turning our back on reality; listening to our emotions ushers us into reality. And reality is where we meet God."[1] When we meet God, we do not fear our emotions, but rather embrace them. What might have happened if Cyndi could have honestly acknowledged her disappointment before God instead of turning to stoic acceptance of the situation?

THE GIFT OF EMOTIONS

Often we, like Cyndi, do not recognize that our emotions reflect something about our capacity as God's image bearers. Each of us has been created with a living soul that has the capacity to respond to life's circumstances with joy, laughter, sorrow, tears, and other employed emotions. God created us to give visible and verbal expression to what we experience. When emotive feelings issue from the heart, life is shared. That is why words stemming from felt emotions become powerful in the presence of others.

Emotions are not static. They are triggered by our experiences. This was one of the first indicators that something was terribly wrong in the Garden of Eden. When the man and woman transgressed, they both experienced terrifying sensations of fear and shame, which prompted a series of actions. First they admitted their shame and fear to each other, and then agreed to sew fig leaves for themselves. They felt compelled to hide their negative emotions from the knowledge and reality of God's goodness. Later, when God confronted them, He did not shame them for responding to their emotions. Rather, He used their emotions as a point of reference in the confrontation of their sin. God wanted them to turn to Him when their circumstances triggered emotions.

Life demands responses. Our circumstances or situations may require either a logical, intellectual solution or an emotional response. Often life needs the balance of both. The Proverbs writer instructs us to live with this conceptual balance. He said, "Let not mercy [emotional response] and truth [intellectual response] forsake you" (3:3). An intellectual response alone will often appear harsh and insensitive, while an emotional response alone will often appear weak and inadequate. When intellectual and emotional responses merge, they bring balance and perspective to a situation.

Are there emotions that specifically tag single women over twenty-five? While all women keenly feel the ache of disappointments and broken dreams, older singles, especially, may experience a sense of rejection and abandonment in a way that other women do not. The rejection may be actual or perceived. God vividly illustrated this truth when He gave a descriptive picture of such a woman in Isaiah 54. I call her the Isaiah woman.

THE "ISAIAH WOMAN" PORTRAYED

Isaiah 54 contains a stunning description of the devastation of Israel's beloved city and God's intervention that led to her restoration. God's heart was moved by Jerusalem's dire circumstances and the inhabitants' dreadful plight in exile. In addressing this city, God chose to depict the extremity of the situation by personifying Jerusalem as a disappointed, shattered single woman. In the midst of this great difficulty, God also spoke a message of hope and purpose.

In this account God employed graphic word pictures of the broken woman (city) who had no husband (protector). The raw depiction of the Isaiah woman evokes conflicting emotions as Isaiah paints her barrenness, desolation, disgrace, shame, confusion, reproach, abandonment, rejection, and grief. Her experience is still relevant to single women today. Let's take a look at the Isaiah woman's circumstances of emptiness and rejection and her emotions of shame and grief by first exploring her cultural backdrop.

CULTURAL BACKDROP

In ancient Jewish culture, it was customary for the parents of a young man to select a bride for their son. Tradition demanded that the young woman leave her own family and join her husband's clan. "Thus upon her marriage, a young woman would be thought of as increasing the efficiency of her husband's family and diminishing that of her parents. Therefore, a young man [that] expect[ed] to get possession of their daughter must be able to offer some sort of adequate compensation."[2] The compensation became known as a dowry that the young man offered to the bride's parents. The prospective bride's parents then negotiated with the terms of the proffered dowry until an agreement was reached.

Parents who had more than one daughter were highly interested in having all of their daughters marry. We see this verified in Genesis when Jacob wanted to marry Rachel. Laban, her father, said that her older sister Leah must first be married before Rachel could become Jacob's bride. Under this cultural mindset, two things were of utmost importance. All women were expected to marry and to birth children.

Marriage was not romanticized in ancient culture. Its purpose centered primarily around the establishment of a family and home so that a man's significance and value increased. A wife's significance and worth was defined by her ability or inability to bear sons for her husband. Sons "increase[d] the size, wealth, and importance of the family group or clan."[3] Households considered it a disgrace to have a barren woman in their midst. In ancient Jewish culture, a woman's infertility was seen as a divine curse. If she eventually bore a child, she could rejoice that her reproach was wiped away (Luke 1:25).

Since it was extremely crucial for a woman to produce off-spring, we can understand why the Isaiah woman was intensely agitated with her barren status. The emptiness was twofold, for she had no child to become "'a nourisher of [her] old age'" (Ruth 4:15), and no husband to protect and provide for her (Ruth 3:1). Her identity and worth as a woman was intrinsically wrapped in her fertility and her husband's provision. The Isaiah woman had neither.

EMPTY WOMAN

The Isaiah woman is first introduced as a barren woman. She lived in the awareness of constant emptiness. Her barrenness reflected her deprivation of a husband, children, and a large tent.

She lamented the loneliness of being a single woman. She grieved that no children filled her arms. She cried about the emptiness of her home. Though the Isaiah woman sorrowed about these three things, God offered her hope. He encouraged her to face the emptiness in two most surprising ways.

In the first verse of Isaiah 54, the Isaiah woman is told to sing and cry out as would a pregnant mother. Most newly pregnant mothers rejoice in the knowledge that a baby is in their womb. Mary, the mother of Jesus, responded with a beautiful song to the Lord her Savior (Luke 1:46-55). The second thing a pregnant woman will do is cry out in her labor as she births the child. This is precisely what the Isaiah woman was asked to do in her emptiness. She was to "'break forth into singing, and cry aloud'" (54:1). Her singing and crying out enabled her to embrace the hope that her emptiness would be exchanged for God's fullness.

People are not always aware of the emptiness single women often experience in their lack of a husband, their inability to bear children, and the loneliness of their silent homes. Like the Isaiah woman, single women, too, long for the fullness and completion of marriage, family, and home. Often they just have no platform for admitting these desires. Sometimes cultural expectations assume that only married women can appropriately talk about such things. Other times, even close family and friends are ignorant that such emotions rage within a single's heart, because she never voices her disappointment and emptiness.

What should a single woman do in response to disappointment?

God did not intend her to be a dead end, but rather an enlargement of His kingdom. Her "tent"—her calling, her career, and her home—has boundless opportunities to expand and enlarge in the place of her former emptiness. However, enlargement requires radical trust in God! Often our tendency is to hang on tightly to the little we do have, instead of risking enlargement. We do not feel quite sure we can trust God to take our emptiness and smallness and enlarge our tent without endangering us. In her book, *The Path of Loneliness*, Elizabeth Elliot sums it up like this:

> *Our hesitancy is like that of a tiny shell on the seashore, afraid to give up the teaspoonful of water it holds lest there not be enough ocean to fill it again. Lose your life, said Jesus, and you will find it. Give up, and I will give you all. Can the shell imagine the depth and plentitude of the ocean? Can you and I fathom the riches, the fullness, of God's love?*[4]

God is able to do more than we could ever imagine. He invites us to release our emptiness to His providence. Then we can begin rejoicing in the possibility of birthing beyond ourselves what we are incapable of producing within. An "empty woman" has the noble privilege of focusing without distraction on kingdom work. In God's economy, her emptiness becomes His enlargement within her. There are no boundaries in God's definition of such extensions!

REJECTED WOMAN

The cause of the Isaiah woman's single status is unclear. This woman may have been widowed, as portrayed in Isaiah 54:4. Verse six suggests that she may have experienced the utter rejection and abandonment of a husband who divorced her during the betrothal period. In ancient cultures, the betrothal covenant was a public witness between the bride's and groom's families. The young man was required to give the young woman some article as a notarized commitment that he would marry her. This was almost as binding as their marriage vows a year later.[5] However, it was possible for the young woman to receive a bill of divorcement during this betrothal period, as Joseph considered doing to Mary before the angel intercepted him in a dream (Matthew 1:19).

Whether the Isaiah woman was divorced or widowed or never given in marriage, we do know that she experienced rejection as a single woman. Verse six implies that she was not chosen among others. She was not sought out. She was not loved by another. The Isaiah woman was crushed with the knowledge that no dowry validated her. Her friends walked into marriage and family security while she crouched in a corner of the tent. She was abandoned by others and marked as a rejected woman with a hopeless future.

Rejection is the subtle voice whispering the lie that you don't have what it takes to be loved. This brings to mind a regular occurrence during my high school days. Our upper grade recess activities involved student-directed softball games. After a hurried sack lunch, we gathered on the ball field to choose teams. Two appointed captains then began their player selections. As our names were called, we moved to the captains' sides. Those with the greatest athletic abilities were always chosen first.

No one wanted to be chosen last, for it carried the stigma of inadequate skill. Unfortunately, the same students were usually chosen last. With downcast eyes, they shifted uncomfortably, waiting for the captains to reluctantly call out their names for the teams. These students experienced a subtle form of rejection because they could not produce athletically. They didn't have what it took to be really wanted and loved by the team.

The stakes are far higher in the context (or lack) of committed relationships. A woman's rejection by a man in preference for another woman is probably the most devastating rejection she can ever encounter. She is rejected not for her skills but for her very personhood. That is one of the reasons why divorce is so demoralizing. It is about her as a person. It implies that she is not worth her spouse's energy, his time, his commitment, and his love. In *The Mystery of Marriage*, Mike Mason says,

> *Everything about marriage is personalized—the joy, but also the pain. Marriage is not the sharp corner of a table banging into your side, but a person speaking a sharp word to you. It is not waving your fist into an empty sky, but rather into a human face, into the face of your own love. It is not the graying or the stiffening of muscles: it is the person you love looking at you as if suddenly you are old or ugly or a piece of excess baggage.*[6]

A divorced woman experiences overwhelming pain through the rejection of her spouse, but a single woman may experience similar subtle rejection when her close friends begin dating or marry. The rejection may be compounded by the fact that her friends abandoned her for a significant other. But worse, she is acutely reminded that no man has chosen her to be on his team. As the single woman grows older and single male peers diminish, she can easily assume that she is not worthy of anyone's love and commitment.

What did God say to the Isaiah woman steeped in her rejection? First of all, God acknowledged her rejection and abandonment. Then He promised to be her Redeemer and to call her to Himself with compassion. He promised His faithful care and presence to keep her from walking alone.

God does no less today for His daughter who keenly feels the rejection and abandonment of key women and men in her life. No matter how deep the rejection and how excruciating the abandonment, the Lord God wants her heart exclusively. He will call her into relationship with Himself—that is the very antithesis of rejection! She will no longer be forsaken, but loved by the One who is ever faithful!

SHAMED WOMAN

The Isaiah woman writhed in a searing shame that twisted the reality of her situation. She became focused on comparing herself with others. She was unlike her married peers. She paled in comparison, for she was considered incompetent and incapable. She was not a distinguished woman who had a husband "respected at the city gate" (Proverbs 31:23 NIV). She hung her head and shuffled along in despair.

As people taunted and pointed fingers at the Isaiah woman, shame attacked her with physical manifestations. She broke out in a sweat; her face got hot; she blushed with embarrassment. The monster of scorn ruthlessly attacked this vulnerable, unmarried woman. How can shame be so devastating? According to Webster, shame is "a painful feeling of having lost the respect of others because of the improper behavior, incompetence, etc.

of oneself or another."[7] The Isaiah woman's inability to be like others placed her in a camp of her own, lonely and isolated. She became a woman ignored and rejected because of her inability to perform as others did. In this she was deeply shamed.

God spoke to this victim of shame and said, "'Do not fear, for you will not be ashamed; neither be disgraced, for you will not be put to shame; for you will forget the shame of your youth, and will not remember the reproach of your widowhood anymore'" (Isaiah 54:4). How those words must have soothed and salved her wounded heart, which had borne the scornful taunts of those unlike her!

Single women are acutely aware of the differences between them and their married peers. Pride, the root of shame, tempts us to compare our ability and competence with that of our married peers. The shame of our inadequacies often causes us to steer clear of anything that will reinforce that fear and knowledge. To counter shame, we foster a competitive spirit to prove ourselves worthy. But we cannot eradicate shame by working harder at a job or at relationships. Shame is an intrinsic response when our vulnerability and pride are exposed. Shame can be defied and overcome only by the Person of Him who loves us enough to become our Protector and Redeemer.

There is yet another aspect of shame we should address. The root of shame is our bent toward worshiping something other than the Lord God.

Our culture declares, "Shame arises because I am a victim and I feel bad about myself." The Bible declares, "Shame arises because I am an idolater

> and I feel foolish when my idol topples" ([See]
> Isaiah 44:9, 19-20).
>
> Shame is the divestiture of self-glory. It is the
> loss of the god—the extension of the self—that
> holds our world together. Shame is an experience
> of being exposed as a fool.[8]
>
> Idolatry is sneaky worship. It is worship of the self,
> but it doesn't look that way at first. It appears
> more like a poor self-image. Or it looks like an
> insecurity that necessitates always looking good,
> or never making mistakes or determination to be
> successful.[9]

As singles, our identity outside the normal expectations of marriage and family can produce many moments of discomfort, especially in social settings. We feel shame when thoughtless remarks are directed toward us. We are tempted to react negatively and enter social interactions cautiously. Our response to and discomfort with singlehood easily turns us inward, and we live as victims. We are hindered from seeing our subtle determination to be someone deserving of validation and credibility. This is a self-worship.

When we as women feel the emotion of shame, it is a call to turn away from an idolatrous heart that is worshiping self. Shame becomes a voice that invites us to fix our eyes on Jesus. In our worship of His glory, we become God-focused, and shame's power and bondage are broken.

GRIEVED WOMAN

The Isaiah woman never once placed her foot inside the door of stoicism. Instead, she walked with an open face and open heart in the wake of her disappointment and pain. Her feelings of grief paralleled her feelings of shame. We read of her as a woman "'grieved in spirit'" (Isaiah 54:6). The King James rendering implies that this grief was a deep-seated, ongoing sorrow. This grief fabricated and carved her identity as a vulnerable woman. She couldn't just get over her grief and go on as though everything was fine.

Her grief was akin to what the Psalmist expressed when he said, "I am weary with my groaning; all night I make my bed swim; I drench my couch with my tears. My eye wastes away because of grief; it grows old because of all my enemies" (Psalm 6:6-7). The Isaiah woman was not reluctant to lament and mourn her single status and its deprivation and losses. She did not hold in her emotions with feigned propriety and piousness. No! She cried out as did Job, "My friends scorn me; my eyes pour out tears to God" (Job 16:20).

We as women are bent on making life *work* for our comfort and satisfaction. When we can no longer dictate a world of comfort, we grieve. Grieving is an expression of loss. Grieving can turn one inward and lead to depression. Godly grief learns to focus not on self, but on God and His purposes. We learn something about ourselves and God in the house of mourning that we don't learn in the house of feasting (Ecclesiastes 7:2). Sorrow mellows and redirects our bent toward independence and arrogance.

I wonder if all childless, single women are called at some

point in their lives to grieve that their bodies are not producing as they were designed to. Grieving is admitting inadequacy to change things and make them as they should be in this world. That is God's job. When we singles grieve our disappointments and losses, we make room for God and others to enter our lives. Grief empties. Grief empowers. Grief cleanses the swollen pride, the petulant demands, and the selfish ambitions from our hearts. When we admit our emptiness and need, we can receive God's mercy and be empowered by His love.

MORE STORIES

All women have experienced emptiness and rejection at some level. The emotions of vulnerable shame and grief have crouched at our doorsteps. We have cuddled the lie that we lack worth and beauty. We have wrongly believed our unworthiness for love. We have circled around the whirlpools of self-pity. These thoughts-hinged-on-emotions eventually lead to the absorption of negative thought patterns, causing us to wallow in the quagmire of despair.

Godly grief embraces loss and deprivation with eyes of faith in the divine sovereignty of God. Faith recognizes Him as Jehovah-jireh, "'The-Lord-Will-Provide'" (Genesis 22:14). His provisions are more than adequate for my situation, no matter how devastating that situation may be. What does godly lament look like? Let us take a few examples of women from Scripture who struggled with emptiness and rejection. How did godly grief, or the lack of it, impact their outcome?

HANNAH

Hannah stared at the children scampering around the tethered animals. She whimpered brokenly, hugging her empty arms to herself. Her eyes swept the tent's provisions. Hannah did not lack as a wife. She was married to a man who loved her as his own soul and gave her all she needed and more. However, Hannah had a private grief: those children belonged to another woman. Her own body was barren. She yearned for the one thing that her husband Elkanah could not create for her—a baby.

They had made their yearly trek to Shiloh and set up camp. Once again, Elkanah had been generous to her in preparation for their sacrifices. He had given to Hannah a greater portion than he did to Peninnah and the sons she had borne him. Although Hannah was loved by her husband, she had no fruit, no witness of their union. Adding wound upon wound, Peninnah's condescending attitude toward her made it especially difficult for Hannah.

In bitterness of soul, she came to the end of herself. Hannah left the tent and walked to the tabernacle to talk to God. Sobs wracked her young body as she lifted up empty hands and arms. Eyes closed, she turned her wet face upward, mouthing her silent petition. She admitted that she had nothing and could produce nothing without divine intervention. She vowed that if God would grant the desire of her heart, she would give the child back to Him.

I doubt that Hannah was bargaining with God in that prayer or vow. Rather, it seems, she had come to the end of herself and had given what only she could give. She offered a broken self and the dream of a son. Her prayer echoed a submission similar to a prayer that Thomas à Kempis prayed, "As thou wilt; what thou wilt; when thou wilt."[10] Her submission freed her to hold out open hands in requesting the gift of a child. She understood that she was not deserving of any of God's gifts and that ultimately all gifts belong to Him.

Why does God sometimes wait to move on behalf of His children? We may not always know. Perhaps there is a work of trust He must first perform in our hearts. It is doubtful that Hannah would have considered giving her firstborn to God had she not first walked the path of barrenness that led her to the path of submission. She enlarged her heart in her barrenness, and offered to God the tears of submission that would water the fruit of her fullness.

ESTHER

The young female outcast gasped as she bowed her head to receive her royal crown. Rising, she flashed a radiant smile and gentle eyes at her lovely attendants standing close by, also attired in royal garments. In another moment they would move from the throne room to the banquet hall and celebrate this momentous occasion. Of all the women contestants, Esther had been the chosen queen for Ahasuerus, who resided in Susa, a city of the Persian Empire.

Esther and her cousin Mordecai were Israelites from the tribe of Benjamin. Their families had been taken captive and carried into Jewish exile during Nebuchadnezzar's reign. Now, Esther and Mordecai were willing to be used by God in royal positions for the deliverance of their people, the Jews, who were about to be annihilated by an enemy. God could use Esther because she had learned to trust Him before she ever attained the royal position of queen.

Esther's background was far from glamorous. Residing in a foreign country with neither father nor mother, Esther had been thrust into the care of a relative. As a single lady, she was dependent on Mordecai. She experienced the tension of being a foreigner in a city that mocked the Jewish culture and identity. She could identify with loss and disappointment. The odds were stacked against her, but they did not produce sallow eyes and a bitter heart. Esther was described as a "lovely and beautiful" woman (Esther 2:7). Her inner beauty synchronized with her physical beauty because she had learned to trust Mordecai and God.

She displayed that trust when she went before the king to beg the life of her people. Could she have been sure of his love and affection since he had not seen her in the last thirty days? She faced him in all her vulnerability as a woman. We read that she "pleaded with the king, falling at his feet and weeping. She begged him to put an end to the evil plan of Haman the Agagite" (Esther 8:3 NIV). In bringing all of her heart, she brought deliverance to her beloved people. Her sorrow made it possible for much rejoicing some days later.

At a casual glance, Esther's story may appear as a fairytale dream. Her good fortune seems to have dropped, random and unwarranted, into her lap. There is more than meets the eye. Do you think she thought it good fortune to be chosen by a king who had spent many nights with other women? Sharing the king's bed prior to marriage was in direct opposition to Esther's faith and a violation to her womanhood.

Could Esther have risen to glory had she not learned to embrace her circumstances and disappointments with an unflinching trust in God? Could her circumstances have changed if she had not embraced the desire for something better? She did not demand change, but asked instead for mercy in her difficult situations.

Can you bring your heart to the Father in your difficult circumstance as a single? Desire much. Ask much. What is your need; what is your request? How badly do you want change? Complacency never brings deliverance. When we bring all of our heart to the Father, void of demand, He will intervene in ways we never dreamed possible.

LOT'S DAUGHTERS

Tension hung in the air as Lot's oldest daughter turned the venison on the spit. The acrid smoke stung her eyes as she loosened her veil in the warming sun. She glanced at her father's turned back as she prepared his breakfast. She wiped a hand across her forehead, trying to forget his accusing eyes. *Well*, she thought defiantly, *what does Father expect us to do in this God-forsaken place? Are we to be single all our lives? How does he expect his posterity to perpetuate if we don't do something about it?*

Her attention was diverted by her younger sister coming back with more firewood. The older hastily mouthed to the younger, "Father knows." The younger sister's glance toward the slumped figure left her in no doubt that Lot was unhappy about their situation.

Neither am I happy, the youngest thought bitterly. *My sister and I are both carrying a child from him, but what could we do? We didn't choose to be chased out of the city to this hole in the mountain. What man would have found us in this stinking cave?*

Many years earlier, Lot had made an unwise decision that led to the demise of his wife and his future in-laws. He had moved into a city that God later destroyed for its wickedness. God's merciful hand had led Lot, his wife, and his two single daughters to escape an outpouring of fire and brimstone. As they fled, Lot's wife looked back and became a pillar of salt. Lot and his two daughters escaped to a small city called Zoar. Afraid he would not be safe in this little burg, Lot took his two daughters on to make their home in a mountain cave.

How did Lot and his unmarried daughters make the transition from a plush lifestyle to a crude, dark cave? It was a sad plight indeed! His daughters reeled under many losses. Their mother had become a salt monument. Their plans for marriage had disappeared in flames. The oldest daughter concluded that the future held no promise. She felt compelled to fix the problem of their family line coming to an abrupt end.

Instead of bringing their sorrow before the God of Abraham, these distressed single women took matters into their own hands. Logic offered a solution to their dilemma. They reasoned that they could use their father to bear children. The family lineage was preserved through an incestuous relationship. These sons later became the fathers of the Moabites and the Ammonites, both of whom became bitter enemies of Israel.

The Bible preserves the sobering example of these two young women who despaired, but did not bring their lament before the Lord. They did not grasp the truth that God could be trusted.

Did they not remember that He had intervened for them in the city? Could they not trust Him to come to their aid in the cave? Many of us can identify with Lot's daughters in our seemingly hopeless circumstances. When we face disappointments, we feel driven to do something about them. Our logic leads us to bad places! God longs for us to bring our anxious hearts to Him and lay the matter before Him. When we rest in His wisdom and providence, God will show up. He always does.

OPEN DOORS, SHUT DOORS, AND THE BORDERS BEYOND

Hannah, Esther, and Lot's daughters had a commonality of very difficult circumstances. Their circumstances produced fear, shame, rejection, distress, and tears. Yet the women's responses varied, and so did the end results.

Like these four women, we will face life difficulties, and our responses matter! They will define our destiny. Faith is demonstrated when we embrace our losses and bring our laments before the Father. In so doing, we give Him an opportunity to move on our behalf, and lead us to a place of fullness and glory.

I recall one dark night when I realized that one of my life dreams, the desire for children of my own flesh and blood, would not come to pass except by a "Sarah" miracle. When I entered my forties-decade, I knew my biological clock was on borrowed time. Yet I still hoped, prayed, and longed to have at least one baby, if not three, to carry in my womb and then birth. I became alert to the occasional news stories of forty-year-old mothers and articles on the risks of having babies at that age. I hoped to be one of the success stories. But time moved on. I was fast approaching the fifties, and I still was not married, and I had no children.

As I sat on my bed that definitive night, knowing my chances were over, I began weeping gut-wrenching sobs. In my sorrow, I brought my lament before the Lord and sat in His presence grieving that my yearning for a child could never be fulfilled on this earth. After a few moments of uncontrollable weeping, the heaviness of God's presence descended into the room, quieting my sobs. I knew God had come near. He spoke most lovingly these gentle words into my consciousness, "It will be okay." I could only sit in awe. In that moment I knew that God had firmly closed the "Door to Children" in my life. I also knew that this was not the end, for He never closes one door without opening another.

No matter how much I pound, cry, scream, and kick, I cannot open the door I have eyed for many years. God has closed it with finality, and He holds the key. For reasons undisclosed, He has chosen not to open the "door" of my womb. However, having no children of my own is not the end of the story! He summons me toward the open door leading to "Childlessness" and beckons me to enter. I have a choice. In my disappointment, can I submit to the Father's sovereign plan and walk through the door He lovingly holds open for His purposes and glory? It is only in my submission to His call that my tears, like those of the Isaiah woman, will water the fruition of a dream far larger than life, and my laments will turn into a song of triumph and glory.

Despite the distressing circumstances the Isaiah woman faced, she was called to envision something beyond the reality of her own limitations. She was summoned to reach beyond confinement—by her songs in barrenness, by her enlargement of an empty tent, and by her trust in God, her Protector and Provider. Let's explore how we too, as single women, are invited to defy the odds in our lives with songs, with enlargements, and with trust in a God who compassionately calls the forsaken and grieved woman to Himself.

chapter eight

ENLARGING YOUR TENT

My parents have come to be known for their generosity and gracious hospitality. They frequently, willingly share their resources and time with others. One day in my teenage years they picked up Ellie, an older single, who needed a ride to the same social event our family was attending. A friendly, petite lady with striking facial features, Ellie readily joined in conversation as we cruised down the interstate. When the discussion flitted around marriage, she suddenly focused on me and lightly teased me about getting married someday.

I figured that Ellie was quite eligible for marriage too. If she would not do it soon, she might miss out on this lifetime adventure. With great hope for her future, I responded sincerely, "Maybe you will get married someday too, Ellie!"

She shook her head decisively and said, "I am too old to get married. Marriage is not for me." Even though I disagreed with her, for Ellie, it was the end of the discussion.

Unfortunately, as the years passed Ellie grew more inward focused and less flexible. Opinionated and suspicious of other people's motives, she retreated into the safety of her own world.

She held secrets of her past that only those closest to her knew in sketchy detail.

Although Ellie is no longer living, I still wonder about her experience as a single lady. What were her dreams and goals in her twenties? What were her relational challenges and disappointments? Had she aspired to stay single all her life? How did she find fulfillment in singlehood? Should she have risked more?

MORE THAN MEETS THE EYE

The breadth and depth of a woman's influence and calling depends on the risks she takes in the face of her uncertain future. Ellie limited her life by closing the door to anyone who threatened the safety of her vulnerable heart. Unless a woman humbly turns to God in her vulnerability, she becomes a prime candidate for bitterness. Bitterness shrinks our hearts, reduces our possibilities for enlargement, and dims God's good purposes and intentions for us.

Disappointment can be the impetus for change in our lives. The Isaiah woman faced disappointments. Her tent was too small, her curtains too petite, her cords too short, and her stakes too weak. God encouraged this woman to look at her disappointing limitations not as dead ends, but as possibilities to make extensions. The human tendency is to focus on temporal extensions. But God's enlargements reach eternal perspectives and boundaries.

God called the Isaiah woman to lift her eyes to the eternal.

> *"Do not fear, for you will not be ashamed; neither be disgraced, for you will not be put to shame; for*

*you will forget the shame of your youth, and will
not remember the reproach of your widowhood any
more. For your Maker is your husband, the LORD
of hosts is His name; and your Redeemer is the
Holy One of Israel; He is called the God of the
whole earth"(Isaiah 54:4-5).*

God was not promising provision by a physical marital union,
but He did promise a marriage: connection and completion with
Him through Christ and the Holy Spirit.

The good news is that a single woman does have a place in
this world, and she is not alone! As single women, we are Christ's
help meet, although not because He is incapable of accomplish-
ing a work, or because He is lacking in some area. Rather, He
calls us to be His privileged handmaidens for a larger purpose
than our own fulfillment. He asks us to willingly offer our gifts
and abilities so that His kingdom will be enlarged. Like the Isaiah
woman, the Lord God asks us single women today to stretch the
boundaries of our tents to include our families, our churches,
our communities, our world, and our worship.

ENLARGING YOUR TENT THROUGH
RELATIONSHIPS AND SERVICE

Let me say it again: "Being a single woman is not the end of
the story!" It is only the beginning of something very wonderful
that God will bring to completion. God never leaves His work
unfinished. He longs for us to see that we are His privileged
daughters, equipped to serve in capacities that married people
would find encumbering.

As single women, we must recognize that it is not in the physical reality that our fullness dwells, but in the life of the Lord Jesus Christ. "'For in Him we live and move and have our being'" (Acts 17:28). When we grasp this truth, we can come alongside the Isaiah woman and take inventory of our tent too. Perhaps as you look at your limitations, you don't even know where to start making changes. The enlarging of a tent sounds hopeful, and being married is an exciting dream, but how does an unmarried woman live in the fluidity of worship and growth? Let's explore this more in practical ways.

ENLARGING YOUR TENT WITH CHILDREN

When a woman does not have children of her own, I believe she is given a greater capacity to open her heart to all children. I see this in my own experience. My sisters and sisters-in-law have families of their own. Their maternal instincts seek to love and care for their own children in ways they do not for their nieces and nephews. They are not erring in some way, but rather living in response to their God-given design. They were created to encircle the precious children from their own womb.

As a single woman, my maternal instincts have made me look beyond myself. Childlessness opens my heart to the children within my sphere of relationships. This is not saying my sphere is greater or lesser; it is just different from that of married women who have children. For this reason each of my nieces and nephews holds a special place in my heart. Treasuring them has helped to alleviate the ache in the lack of my own children. I also have had the privilege of enjoying them without the strain and hard work of training them.

Just as parenting styles look different, I believe "aunting" styles vary as well. A few of my single friends pile their nieces and nephews into a vehicle and take them on a mini-vacation once a year. One summer I was nanny for my brother's children while he and his wife attended a music school in Nashville for a week. The children and I explored parts of the city and thoroughly enjoyed our time together. A few of my summers were spent in northwestern Ontario with another brother and his family. During that time I made each of his four young children a personalized story book of photos I had taken of them.

If you have only a few nieces and nephews, you might consider Carolyn McCulley's idea. As a single author, she wrote:

> *I have an "Aunt's Journal" for each of them [nieces and nephews], in which I am writing to their future adult selves with observations and memories of our times together in their childhoods. I look forward to the day I give these faded, yellowed journals to them. I hope these books will kindle memories for them and reinforce my affection for each one.[1]*

The ideas are limitless. You might entertain them with your interests by sleepovers, campouts, shopping excursions, sports, or tea parties. Your time with them will create memories and impressions that will have lasting impact.

One thing we dare not forget is the degree of influence a single aunt can have. "The Lord has placed our nieces and nephews in our lives for a purpose. We have the opportunity to make an investment in these children through time, affection, counsel, and encouragement."[2] I have made it a habit to attach each niece and nephew to a certain day of the week and to pray for them on that specific day. In this small way, I hope to touch their lives eternally while also blessing them in their present callings.

Whether or not you have nieces and nephews, involve your life with children. Take notice of your neighbors' children or a church family whom you might unofficially adopt as your own. Sam and Marie, a childless couple, had many nieces and nephews. They found it difficult to know how to lavish attention on just a few of them without seeming partial. They were attracted to a newly wedded bride who had left her home and family to move into their locality. They offered the bride and her husband their parental affection and guidance. With time, the young couple's children became Sam and Marie's unofficially-adopted grandchildren. This special connection between two families was a lifelong relationship and blessing.

The stories could go on and on of selfless, childless single women who have touched the lives of many children. These stories are not just limited to the biographies of Gladys Aylward, Amy Carmichael, Annie Funk, Mary Slessor, and Mother Teresa. They also include thousands of women who have quietly blessed the lives of children in their own locale, or around the world through various organizations. When single women invest their time and energy with children, they enlarge their tents in ways they never could as a mother of biological children.

ENLARGING YOUR TENT FOR YOUR SIBLINGS

We single women sometimes underestimate our value or discredit our impact with our biological (and adopted) families. Our tendency is to compare what we don't have with what they have. This threatens our single status, and we become competitive or jealous of married siblings. Peevish or critical attitudes affect our relationships and limit our freedom to give spontaneously to our siblings.

Negative attitudes toward your siblings sprout as tiny rootlets. They may start with something as small as a sibling's insensitivity of your placement at the family dinner table or family gathering. Since you are the unpaired adult, they place you where it would be more inconvenient for a couple. Maybe you find yourself annoyed by their careless comments about your free time, or their expectation that you can do more. Other times you may feel used as a convenient babysitter because your lifestyle is not hampered by your own family unit.

In our disappointment, do we demonstrate petulance and self-pity when our family does not serve us perfectly in something we deem important? Do our attitudes play a big role in the way we are treated as single women? Who are you as a person with your family? Do you love well? Do you give well? Do you receive well? If we cannot answer these questions in the affirmative, we can hardly expect anything but the same measure returned to us.

Even though we are not married, our interactions with our siblings can teach us the virtue of selflessness. This character quality is demanded of every godly wife and mother I know. A mother can hardly make her family revolve around her needs; she revolves around the needs of her family. Her love is sacrificial. She is constantly required to lay down her own desires for the sake of her family and their needs.

The propensity toward inflexibility is a fault of older single women. They don't have to practice daily selflessness and sacrificial love like a woman in a healthy marriage does. As sisters in Christ, and as sisters in our biological families, we single women are called to the same quality of selflessness. We can practice this selflessness with our siblings. They honestly reflect who we are and who we are not. Our humility in giving in to their requests and receiving their honest opinions will keep us soft and pliable.

What I have called selflessness, Elizabeth Elliot called oblation. She said, "My theme is oblation—the offering up of ourselves, all we are, have, do, and suffer. Sacrifice means something received and something offered."[3] Some women have received singlehood. How is that offered as a sacrifice to the Lord? We can begin by asking ourselves how our singlehood can serve our immediate family. We are not asking, "Why are they not blessing me?" Rather we ask, "How can I bless my family, including my married siblings?" Affirmation, encouragement, and assistance are three primary ways we single women can bless our siblings.

AFFIRMATION, ENCOURAGEMENT, ASSISTANCE

A basic need for all siblings is the verbal affirmation of one another's gifts and abilities. Why is it so difficult to validate each other through words? Members of a family tend to be broken in the same places. This makes it difficult to speak into each other's

lives without feeling threatened and criticized. We diffuse sibling
tension and rivalry when we begin blessing and validating with
little or no expectation that it be reciprocated.

"Marriage and children take work and wisdom and dependence on God. There's really nothing romantic about it."[4]
Since my youngest sister is twelve years younger than my
youngest brother, she was continually "behind" her siblings—
stuck in a stage long after they were past it. Even as an adult,
at times she lamented her feelings of inadequacy as a parent
when she observed her older siblings on the top side of raising
their families. Any words of encouragement from her siblings
watered her soul as a young mother.

We single women, especially, have the freedom to be liberal
in our encouragement and praise because we don't have families
vying for our attention. Words empower and have amazing
results. "Pleasant words are a honeycomb, sweet to the soul and
healing to the bones" (Proverbs 16:24 NIV).

We feel validated when someone takes the time to listen to
us. We hunger for such closeness. Yet often those closest to us do
not notice our need. It is not surprising, then, that we bitterly
complain about our siblings who focus only on their own families.
Let's flip the coin. Our married siblings also need listening ears.
They encounter job issues, marriage issues, child issues, and relational issues. Sometimes the safest place to talk about these
things is with the single relative who has no spouse or children
to threaten or be threatened by that sharing platform. Here is
an opportunity to practice selflessness and come alongside as an
encourager.

Single women can also bless their siblings by offering

assistance in the demands of life. We can assist with lawn and garden care, babysitting, food preparation, or a house project. "But I don't have time!" you may argue. We do not have more time than our married siblings. We all are given a precious twenty-four hours each day. Probably we are not even less busy than our married siblings; however, our schedules often have more flexibility. Families must combine the schedules of multiple people, but a single woman has one schedule. This frees us to be more flexible. Give liberally of your time and energy in serving your siblings, and the returns will multiply!

ENLARGING YOUR TENT FOR YOUR PARENTS

As single women, what should we offer our parents? They certainly are deserving of our expressions of gratitude. Some of us might feel negative about our parents and home life. But remember—even in the most dysfunctional homes, parents do not set out to become failures. Nor do they intend to produce an unstable or troubled home. Your parents had high hopes as they walked to the marriage altar. Most of us do not reckon with an enemy who is at war with marriage and family. For this reason we stand as much in need of God's grace as do our parents, no matter what our home situation.

For a moment, let us put aside all negative thoughts we have accumulated about our parents through the years. Let's think about the first twelve years of our lives. Imagine all the work that we as infants demanded from our mothers. As children, who clothed us? Who laundered our clothes? Who fed us? Think about the meals that were prepared in those twelve years:

approximately 13,140! If our mothers or fathers did only two loads of laundry for us each week, they did 1,250 loads in twelve years for just one person. We likely had a parent or provider who went to work every day so we would have a roof over our heads and bread on the table. Aren't they deserving of some kind words?

As we grow older, so do our parents. Think of ways you can assist them. Maybe you could drive for them, or mow their lawn, or help with general housework. Cooking is not my mother's favorite domestic duty. When I go home, I often take over in the kitchen. She has commented with relief more than once, "I don't worry about meals when you are at home." Try to discover your parents' needs. Attempt to relieve their stress level, not out of a sense of duty, but rather out of a heart of gratitude.

Should a single woman feel responsible for the care of her elderly parents, since she does not shoulder the responsibility for a family? Ideally, this would be something a single woman and her siblings could mutually agree upon. Even though she might be more flexible, she is her own breadwinner too. Perhaps that needs to be given some consideration, but income should not be the only factor in the final conclusion. A single woman's choice to reciprocate parental love and care is indeed a noble, selfless gesture.

ENLARGING YOUR TENT WITH YOUR CHURCH AND COMMUNITY

Single women can make significant contributions to the local church. One need not be married to do this. Far too often, single women assume a passive role in the local church. I am often reminded of Phebe, a single woman who carried a letter for Paul. She left Cenchreae, a seaport of Corinth, and traveled to Rome to deliver a letter we know as the Book of Romans (Romans 16:1-2). It is likely that she walked north to Macedonia and then took a boat to cross the Adriatic Sea to reach Italy. From there, she probably walked again until she reached Rome.

This trip required not only time, but also physical stamina and incredible risks. The point is that Phebe was willing to be used of God for the work of His kingdom. We don't know what happened to her after her letter was delivered, but we can draw conclusions based on what we know.

> *If Phebe returned to Corinth, we can know she went right on being Phebe, God's woman. If she stayed in Rome, the same. God Himself was Phebe's home, and the ground on which she stood was holy ground. She did not demand to choose her scene of service; she served where she was, knowing He [the Lord God] was there too...* [5]

Phebe enlarged her tent by risking unfamiliar terrain to do a robust work that a married woman of her day could not do.

Single women, like Phebe, have gifts they can offer to their church and community. We might say, "Oh, but I don't have any gifts! I can't bake like Jean, and I don't have the financial security Heidi does." Yet we all have something we can do and something we can give. One place to start is to look at your interests. Do you enjoy baking, cooking, sewing, reading, cleaning, teaching, clubs, children, teenagers, elderly people, or committees? From there, discover ways to expand your world by sharing and blessing people with these gifts.

I recognize that sharing resources with others requires spending additional time and money. God's liberal hand does not run dry when we give in His name and for His service. Jesus said our lifestyle should be one of giving, and then His provisions would come in (Luke 6:38). We often get this idea reversed! We want to give once we acquire "enough" provisions and resources.

As godly single women, we are responsible to be wise stewards of our finances. We also have the freedom to make choices in our giving, in agreement with God's Spirit. Most often, we err on the side of self-protection. My maternal grandmother taught me much about giving. With limited assets and an income below poverty level, she still freely tucked ten- and twenty-dollar bills in unexpected places to bless people. Amazingly, she never ran out of money. At the time of her death, she left funds not only for funeral expenses, but also a small amount to bless each of her twelve children.

There are many ways to give creatively! Ask the Holy Spirit for direction. Try doubling your tip the next time you go out to eat. You don't have a child to clothe or feed, but perhaps your waitress does. It will lighten her load and bless her day when she sees the gratuity on her table. Send your money to trustworthy organizations that will help other people in need. Instead of going on your third pleasure trip, share your money with a family who has never been able to afford a vacation. Giving freely of your resources protects you from becoming enslaved to your own interests and needs.

If there is any spiritual gift that will greatly impact and bless the local church and community, it is time spent in prayer! I recall one evening leaving the home of an older single lady, Miss Christner. As my friend and I stepped outside her door, she began praying the Levitical blessing over us (Numbers 6:24-26). I was touched by the sincerity and spontaneity of her prayer. I have never forgotten this single woman's obedience to the Holy Spirit's prompting that evening.

Anna, a widowed woman, didn't leave the temple, but spent her time praying and fasting (Luke 2:36-37). She is an example of the wonderful opportunity single women have to become prayer warriors. We don't have the responsibility of putting children to bed in the evening or getting them up in the morning. Use that time to pray for the families near to you. By default, we single women often find ourselves driving alone—this too is a time when we can send our petitions and praise to the Father's throne (Revelation 5:8). Our aloneness makes it possible to spend uninterrupted time in prayer to the Father through His Spirit.

I believe our prayers will touch people in ways we may never know this side of heaven. Imagine! We single women can spread our prayer tent all over the world! I often wonder when I get Home whether Jesus will say, "Look over there, daughter. See that child...woman...man...? They were touched by your prayers."

ENLARGING YOUR TENT WITH
CAREER AND VOCATIONAL CHOICES

I have talked to many single women who hesitate to set life goals because they don't know how to merge their dreams with their desire for marriage. Sometimes the reluctance is born of a fear that being proactive with their goals indicates they are signing away marriage and family opportunities. Author Evelyn King Mumaw wrote,

> *Until you can get beyond thinking of our singleness as merely an interim stage before marriage, you are in no position to live fully and thus become a woman at her best. When a woman can accept singleness as her particular status, then she can begin to explore its possibilities for life fulfillment; she can live vibrantly* **in the now** *of her life.*[6] [Emphasis added.]

Goals give definition, direction, and purpose. They do not have to be set in stone, and they can be revisited and revised. Consider making goals that encompass all of your life. This could include job and career choices, ministry goals, personal development, social and relational expansion, spiritual growth, and financial plans. Another place to begin with goal setting is to think of your dreams for life accomplishments. Make a list of things you want to do within your lifetime. Finally, make incremental goals of one, five, and ten years stating what you envision and how you plan to arrive there with God's help.

You might question how goals and God's will merge. Our desires, interests, and passions are not born in a vacuum. They spring from God's loving intentions and purposes for our lives. Why would God's will for our lives direct us to do something we have no passion or heart for?

God made us volitional beings. He expects us to make life choices. Do we perhaps have the wrong focus when we ask, "What is God's will for my life?" I wonder if our focus should turn to a question He may be asking: "What will you choose to do with the desires and interests I have placed in your heart? How will you use them to advance My kingdom?" Waiting for a big revelation about God's will for my life is far too often rooted in passivity or fear. We do not have to stall in making life choices. If we make an unwise decision, goal, or commitment, God can stop us and turn us around.

Perhaps we find it difficult to know how our interests will align with a career choice or ministry calling. Career, personality, or compatibility tests and checklists can provide broad-range parameters for vocational and ministry choices.

Thinking about things you enjoyed doing as a child can give assistance in defining your life's direction. Any one of these has possibilities for you as an adult. Were you a leader? Did you enjoy numbers? Did you love animals? Did you work with food? Were you an outdoor person? As a child, I enjoyed playing school and hospital with my siblings. In retrospect, I see it was not only the professionalism that intrigued and delighted me, but also the organization it took to create the setting. Not surprisingly, my career choice led me to the classroom.

Pursuing careers based on our interests powerfully impacts our service to the Lord. Passionate, fulfilled people, serving in capacities that enlarge their hearts, will make significant contributions to God's kingdom!

LOOKING BEYOND

Women do experience unrealized dreams, disappointed hopes, and frustrated expectations. We must see life as a journey of faith. Leaning into the faith process is a lifetime endeavor. My dear grandmother, a widow for over twenty years, understood something of this process. She occasionally stated, "Once we know all there is to know, we are finally ready to die." She meant that it takes a lifetime to learn the essentials about relationships and walking with God. When we finally have gained some understanding, we have a limited amount of time to put it into application.

Life processes are intended to make us holy and virtuous daughters of God. He will do what it takes to gain our hearts. Often the path includes the excruciating companions of Sorrow and Suffering, like those the Shepherd brought to Much-Afraid in *Hinds' Feet on High Places*. Like Much-Afraid, we initially resist walking alongside these companions. Hopefully in time we discover that these companions are not enemies, but rather have been transformed into companions of Joy and Peace by the power of the cross.[7]

Changing our perspective and focus from the temporal to the eternal, we now find it possible to turn our hearts from lament to worship. When single women turn toward godly worship, they are enlarging their tents in the face of childlessness and loss. Their worship leaps with joy, skips over mountains, and stakes beyond the boundaries, for nothing can hold back the enlargement of God's kingdom.

ENLARGING YOUR TENT THROUGH WORSHIP

Godly lament loosens the hardness of our hearts. It reveals truth about our situations. It invites Christ and His Holy Spirit to enter our anguish. Godly lament is intrinsically supported by the attitudes of meekness and brokenness and asks God and others for their assistance in our distresses. Asking produces humility. Humility then moves our hearts toward gratitude and worship of a good God. Our vertical worship empowers us to receive His grace and mercy.

Horizontal worship is spawned from a determination to meet the emptiness of one's own needs as did the woman at the well. Men became the object of her worship. Jesus told this promiscuous woman what kind of worship the Father really desires. "'The hour is coming, and now is, when the true worshipers will worship the Father in spirit and truth; for the Father is seeking such to worship Him. God is Spirit, and those who worship Him must worship in spirit and truth'" (John 4:23-24).

To worship Him in spirit is to center all of our heart, including our emotions, in the very character and goodness of the Father. To worship Him in truth is to align all our thoughts and actions with Christ. These two ideas forge a powerful definition of worship. Worshiping in spirit and truth opens the heart to repentance, silence, gratitude, and obedience. Such worship springs out of a heart that seeks to be enlarged by God Himself.

WORSHIP THAT PLEASES GOD

Worship in Repentance

The door of worship unlocks when we repent of our demand that life revolves around us. We often ask, "Why me? Why am I single and my friends are married? Why do I not have a family? Why does she have a husband for the second time, while I have not been married once?" Are these questions the result of wounded pride that is attached to personal fulfillment? We subtly believe we deserve far more than we have, and far more than our situation warrants. Often this attitude is couched in our ideas of fairness. In the words of author Philip Yancey, "The Cross of Christ may have overcome evil, but it did not overcome unfairness. For that, Easter is required. Someday, God will restore all physical reality to its proper place under His reign."[8]

Do you remember Job's reactions to his difficulties and losses? Initially he entered worshipful lament when he lost almost everything. Later he wallowed in self-pity when things didn't change. He struggled to release his demand that things should operate from his perspective of fairness. In chapter after chapter, he described his defensiveness and resistance.

In the last chapter, Job repented from his self-righteousness. He brokenly confessed, "'I have heard of You by the hearing of the ear, but now my eye sees You. Therefore I abhor myself, and repent in dust and ashes'" (42:5-6). When Job released the demand that God come through on his terms, he met God. In his repentance, Job worshiped and brought sacrifices before the Lord.

Worship in Silence

If godly repentance prepares a heart to worship, waiting in silence before God inspires hope and faith. Silence swings open the door, inviting God to show up. He promised, "'Behold, I stand at the door and knock. If anyone hears My voice and opens the door, I will come in to him and dine with him, and he with Me'" (Revelation 3:20). When God comes to us, He speaks His truth. This allows our hope and faith to rest upon a substantive Word that is not shaken. Many times in Scripture we are called to wait silently and patiently for the Lord (Psalm 37:7). As long as we keep talking and trying to make sense of our marital status, we will not hear God. He has things to say to us about our situation if we wait long enough to listen.

Have you ever tried sitting in silence before the Lord for fifteen minutes with your hands laid open upon your lap? (You might even want to try an hour sometime!) Your silence and open hands symbolically admit that you trust God to speak even though you have no words. Open your mind and your spirit to His Holy Spirit. At times God will speak His truth. Other times He will bring truth through the comfort of His Presence. I have often discovered that His Presence comforts me just as much as His still small voice.

As busy singles and career ladies, we may view solitude as a waste of time. However, worshiping in silence and solitude rejuvenates, empowering us to face the demands ahead. When our hearts are quieted, God shows up in unexpected places in our day.

Worship with Gratitude

We can bring our songs of worship only when our hearts are filled with gratitude. We are instructed as single women to express gratefulness for our childless state. "'Sing, O barren, you who have not borne! Break forth into singing, and cry aloud, you who have not labored with child! For more are the children of the desolate than the children of the married woman,' says the Lord" (Isaiah 54:1). Such singing fills the spiritual womb with uncontainable joy. These songs are not forced, pious attempts to look on the positive side. Rather they are songs that bubble up from a trusting heart whose focus is to glorify the One deserving of all praise and honor.

God is pleased when single women bring their songs before Him in faith. Singing defies disappointments and demonstrates trust. I recall the time I attended a singles' retreat, and we spent time singing together. The vibrancy and power of our singing charged the atmosphere. It was as though heaven and earth hung suspended momentarily and then blended into a surreal, other-worldly time and place. I wonder what happens in the heavenly realm when childless, single men and women join together and worship their Creator for His goodness.

Worship in Obedience

Worship inspires us to live in obedience to God's vision and purpose for our lives. Godly worship submits to God's plan that I offer Him my limited resources and make extensions in His kingdom. The focus turns to God instead of to me and my petty demands.

God invited the Isaiah woman to do just that. As she worshiped, He invited her to walk in obedience to what He envisioned. He didn't want her to live small and indifferent to her limitations. God told her, "'Enlarge the place of your tent, and let them stretch out the curtains of your dwellings; do not spare; lengthen your cords, and strengthen your stakes. For you shall expand to the right and to the left, and your descendants will inherit the nations, and make the desolate cities inhabited'" (Isaiah 54:2-3). Her obedient response to Him empowered the enlargement of her life and worship—enlargement far beyond what she could ever have imagined!

TRUSTING GOD, RISKING ENLARGEMENT

Tent enlargement always is accompanied by risk-taking. Let's think again about the barren Isaiah woman who lived in a small tent with no husband. She was asked to defy all odds and live as a whole woman. Surely her neighbors shook their heads at her eccentricity. Imagine the raised eyebrows when she informed them that she was expecting more children than her married friends. How they shook their heads as she began enlarging her dwelling place! They laughed outright when she informed them that her Husband would be known all over the earth. Yet she was right! Her faith was rooted in truth. God's provision surpassed her expectations, and her life became characterized by fullness and joy.

There are tasks in God's kingdom that require individuals with undivided attention. We have historical evidence that many times God has used the weakness of women to serve in unusual capacities. Someone once said,

> *Many times I have observed single women at work in key positions around the world. I have felt very keenly that God has kept many of the church's finest women single because He had special tasks for them to do that they could not have accomplished as married women with families.*[9]

I do not intend to flaunt a single woman's work as more noble or more spiritual than that of raising a godly family. We all have a calling and place in God's kingdom. Surely we can recognize that some kingdom tasks would be hampered by marriage.

The temptation of remaining in "safe mode" in a well defined groove always lures us to stay small. We must avoid the temptation to live out our days in a museum that only showcases lifelessness. Begin your enlargement by opening your tent flaps. If God can take me as a shy, introverted teenager with little self-confidence and develop me into a confident teacher, then He can do the same for you. Step up in faith and step out in risks!

Taking risks is akin to stepping aboard a wild roller coaster. Once the ride begins, you never know exactly where the next dip, the next curve, the next thrill will occur. Place your hands trustingly in those of Father God, who does know, and go for the ride of your life. There is a bigger world out there that needs your gifts, your service, and your love. They need it now. Enlarge your tent, childless woman; "'the kingdom of God is within you'"! (Luke 17:21).

section three

Embracing God's Pattern

The Single's Life Purpose and Calling

Now may the God of peace Himself

sanctify you completely; and may

your whole spirit, soul, and body be

preserved blameless at the coming of

our Lord Jesus Christ. He who calls

you is faithful, who also will do it.

I THESSALONIANS 5.23-24

chapter nine

THE HEART OF FRIENDSHIP

A co-teacher once shared with me a short story one of her first graders wrote. It is doubtful that this young child understood the profundity of her message concerning relationships.

Once upon a time there was a frog and her name was Mulisu. Mulisu was a very cheerful frog. But one day she wasn't happy at all. The reason she was not happy was because she wanted to get married. She was unhappy for fifteen months. Her mother and father were disappointed.

One day she came home from school very, very happy. Her mother and father were glad this time because they did not like grumpy frogs. She told them about the new boy frog in school. And then she thought that he would be just the right one to marry. But there still would be a problem. She was not old enough to get married yet, 'cause she was only six years old.

So she had to wait and wait until she was at least twenty. She had to have fourteen more birthdays until she would be twenty years old.

*It took a very, very long time, but finally she
got married with the frog.*

We smile at this simplistic, delightful story. We wish all relational problems were so easily solved, just by waiting a few years.
Yet our six-year-old author has something deeper to offer—surprising insight into two internal longings of every woman. We
want to belong to someone special, and we want to be loved
exclusively. The awareness of this lack often produces negative
emotions and alters the countenance, as the young author aptly
illustrated.

The grumpy girl frog became distressed when she perceived
her lack and how it was tied to her happiness and fulfillment.
We see the immediate change in her demeanor after discovering
the boy frog. With amazing clarity, the story's resolution comes
only after intimate bonding to another. Marriage is perceived as
closing forever the gap of longing. Like many of us, this first-
grader did not realize that human intimacy is never enough.
Only God can satisfy our deepest ache of longing.

Yet single or married, we all find ourselves desiring human
friendships, both female and male. Why? Friendships are important. Friendships are God-given. Friendships enrich our lives.
Friendships produce life-giving energy and a sense of belonging. Friendships validate our personhood. Friendships anchor
us and provide a foundational equilibrium. In this chapter we
will address a single woman's need for connection and belonging
through appropriate levels of female and male friendships.

FRIENDSHIP VERSUS RELATIONSHIP

Sometimes friendship and relationship are used interchangeably. We often assume that a relationship is indicative of friendship. Does a relationship always produce a friendship or result from friendship? No, not necessarily. According to Webster, a relationship is "1 the quality or state of being related; connection; 2 connection by blood, marriage, etc.; kinship."[1]

Consider the family unit. A family relationship does not automatically produce friendship bonds. Another example is partnership in a business or career. While friendships may develop through business endeavors, the relationship was initiated by a shared interest in the business. Unfortunately, it is even possible to have a physically intimate relationship with a man or woman without friendship.

Friendship often springs out of some level of relationship, but goes beyond the bare bones of relationship. To be identified as a *friend* is to be loved. The word *friend* has its roots in the Germanic language. Possibly it is derived from the word *frijon*, which means "to love."[2] A healthy friendship does not focus on one's own need for love, but commits to selflessly love another.

THE BIOLOGICAL DOMAIN AND FRIENDSHIPS

A woman is wired to gravitate toward intimacy in both female and male friendships. This often shows up very early in her life. For whatever reasons, the right chemistry between certain personalities automatically bonds two people. My youngest sister acquired a best friendship in first grade that kept right on going through her senior year. Today their life callings and husbands' careers have separated them geographically and culturally, limiting their interaction. Yet these two women in their thirties still remain good friends. Not every woman can boast of such a friendship. Blessed are the women who have and hold such a gift!

What kind of chemistry between two people produces such a lifelong friendship commitment? The human brain has left and right hemispheres that can operate independently of each other. In very general categories, the right brain hemisphere operates with emotional responses and creativity. The logical and calculating responses stem from the left side of the brain. Studies suggest that many males tend to lean strongly toward the left hemisphere, but can operate singularly out of either the right brain or left brain. Most women function primarily from the right side of the brain; however, they also do well operating from both hemispheres simultaneously.

These right and left brain hemispheres have implications for women and their friendships. A woman (relating to friendships out of the right hemisphere) has uncanny perception and insight into her friend's responses or the lack of them. She can quickly size up the emotional temperature of a given situation. Quite often her friendship interactions are based more on emotional assumptions than on logic.

Some years ago I remember reading about a study on the emotional responses of young girls. It indicated that girl infants are more likely to cry if they hear other infants cry.

According to Louann Brizendine, a neuropsychiatrist at the University of California in San Francisco, "the female brain picks up emotional cues, both verbal and nonverbal, more quickly than the male brain. Starting at about age twelve girls put feelings into words more efficiently than boys...Repeating negative thoughts can make not only the injured party but those around her more, rather than less, distressed and angry."[3] These tendencies do not change when girls become adults. They just become more subtle.

A woman's intuitive side overlays her environment with emotional tarps, shrouding the facts that logic would emphasize. While this can fabricate negative results, there are also positive repercussions. The emotional factor enriches and blesses a woman's network of friendships. The emotional renewal women receive from each other better equips them to nurture their families and colleagues. A good cry with a friend, a heart-to-heart talk, or spending time together on a project revitalizes a woman's emotional stability and health. She becomes more whole. She becomes more peaceful. She becomes more trustful. Her emotional hunger is momentarily satiated by reciprocating friendship.

The strong bonding in ladies' friendships forges soul connections. Dee Brestin includes an example in her book, *The Friendships of Women.*

> *When Elliot Engel watched his wife and her best friend say goodbye before a cross country move, he found that their last hugs were so painful to witness: he finally had to turn away and leave the room. He said, "I have always been amazed at the nurturing emotional support that my wife can seek and return with her close female friends... Her three-hour talks with friends refresh and renew her far more than my three-mile jogs restore me. In our society it seems as if you've got to have a bosom to be a buddy."[4]*

Because women often intertwine their souls and hearts with each other, they frequently demand that their male friendships look the same. When single and married women return home after spending time with female friends, they may be tempted to demand the same level of emotional intensity from their dads, brothers, and husbands. Guard against creating unrealistic expectations! When we demand that the significant men in our lives relate to us like our female friends do, we effeminate our men.

LEVELS OF FRIENDSHIP

We were created by a relational God, and He made us relational. God did not intend that men and women go solo in this world. Bonding in friendship is comparable to connecting with God. This is illustrated in a familial relationship we read about in Scripture. After being estranged from his brother Esau for so many years, Jacob returned and faced his wrongdoings. He said to his twin, "'Receive my present from my hand, inasmuch as I have seen your face as though I had seen the face of God, and you were pleased with me'" (Genesis 33:10). We, too, see God's face when our friendships are rooted in godly love and commitment!

There may be times when a single woman, in her desire for a husband, will seek a best friend for unhealthy reasons. In her longing for connection, she becomes driven to fill her void of intimacy. She may then seek to bond deeply with a female friend for that purpose. If the soul bond becomes strong enough, she will depend on the relationship in much the same way a married woman depends upon her husband. Fulfillment in such a friendship is only an illusion. When a single woman has crossed this line in a female friendship, she has shifted to an idolatrous relationship. Satiating one's soul hunger should not be the impetus and purpose for relationships.

What kinds of friendships should single women pursue? Before we answer that question, let's consider levels of friendship. As we operate from these levels, they free us to engage in a variety of friendships that enrich and bless our lives. In our relationships with females and males, we could loosely categorize our friendships at six levels, or six progressive degrees of commitment.

Agape Level

This level of friendship is wide but not personal. In it, you recognize your link to the broad range of humanity. *Agape* love is a God-love that is demonstrated toward all mankind. As His child, you are a friend to all people and for all people. *Agape* love looks upon the human race with respect and honor, recognizing people as God's image bearers. Therefore each person is worthy of kindness and compassion. This level, put at the base of every other friendship level, empowers the giver and recipient to be touched by God in a meaningful interchange of two souls, for however brief or long a time.

Acquaintance Level

This is still a broad level of relating, but narrower than the *agape* level. Acquaintances may be your neighbors or people you meet occasionally at social functions. Your interchange is friendly but reserved. The only common ground is face acquaintance and proximity. You graciously acknowledge each other's presence, but do not find it imperative that a long interchange follow. Conversations might center on current events, general knowledge, or people connections. Sharing at an intimate level would be unwise.

Associative Level

The field narrows a bit more. On this level, you mingle frequently with the same people because of shared interests such as careers, institutions, and churches. There is some established knowledge and commonality in this group, and you enjoy reciprocated interaction. You know general information about your associates' families and aspects of their personal lives. You might explore personal likes and dislikes. Shared conversations are stimulating and encouraging. If someone at this friendship level would leave or become angry with you, it would hurt to some degree. But you are still at the stage where you can disengage without being totally devastated.

Affectionate Level

You now are at a level in which you enjoy bantering camaraderie and soul fellowship with people. Here, key friendships create a common bond and warmth. These people matter greatly to you. You give and receive unconditional acceptance. You feel "at home" with these friends because you know each other's strengths and weaknesses. Additional social times are planned beyond the default social gatherings. Although you dare ask more personal questions, there still remains some level of restraint and mystery within this level of friendship. You call these people your close friends. If you would lose one of these friendships, you would keenly feel the loss and find yourself grieving for some time.

Accessible Heart Level

This level of friendship is limited to a few people who are truly committed to you. You have forged with them a soul and spirit connection in which few secrets are held from each other. These people become significant in your life because of shared experiences and shared history. Your friendships with them may be seasonal or lifelong. But few people can penetrate this tight friendship circle. (These few may function as one group, or may involve personal connections to individual people.) This level is based on deep trust and commitment. You call these people your best friends. Losing a friend at this level would be an intensely raw and shattering blow.

Ardent Level

This level is reserved solely for marriage between male and female. It is the most intimate of levels. You have the capacity to know and to be known in your spirit, soul, and body. At this highest level of friendship, two literally become one. The separation of divorce or death is the actual tearing of whole-hearted, whole-person bonds between two people. Here, a loss is the most devastating and shattering of all.

"Friendship level" terminology is used to help picture proximity, but remember, friendships cannot be fully categorized or packaged. Our levels need fluidity to some degree and are constantly in motion. There are transitional places between categories. Our friends may even move back and forth from one level to another. Each friendship serves its time and purpose. Even at the Accessible Heart Level, a circle of close friendship may change depending on one's geographical relocation, life calling, or demise.

A SHIFT IN FRIENDSHIPS

Single women (and men) have complained to me how betrayed they have felt when their best friend married. In the initial passion of wedded life, the couple may consciously or unconsciously drop past friendships. The couple's need for extended friendship is temporarily silenced in the new knowledge and experience of each other.

Married women have told me that something does shift in their former friendships during that first year or two of adjusting to marriage. It takes time and balance to absorb the dynamics of a husband becoming your best friend, while at the same time grappling with maintaining women friendships at the same level as before. In fact, keeping relationships unchanged during this time is nearly impossible. The immature bride who is consumed with her husband's attention does not sense the need to stay engaged with her female friendships. She may wrongly assume that she has finally found the ultimate relationship. It is unwise for a bride to totally ignore her female friends. Undoubtedly, in a few years she will long for their friendship.

Another common complaint from single women is the shift of loyalties in their married friends. The secrets the two women shared prior to the friend's marriage now become information for the husband as well. Again, an insecure bride may feel the need to share every detail of her friend's secrets with her husband. The young wife establishes her place in marriage by giving her husband all of her heart. She is unsure that she has given all her heart if she withholds details she knows. This is not necessarily wrong. A married woman must keep her husband as the closest confidant she has, and yet at the same time treasure female friendships that do not compete with her marriage.

One time I made a statement that after ten years of marriage, it seems most married women are desperate for female friendships. My married sister, hearing the comment, promptly corrected me. She said, "Sharon, it doesn't even take that much time. I was ready for it long before ten years were up." I also recall one woman telling me that as a young bride there was much to learn in the first year of her marriage friendship. It took time and effort to establish constant togetherness with her husband. She felt no need to give outside of her marriage. However, she admitted the day came when she did need friends beyond her marriage relationship.

So while it is unwise for a bride to ignore her past friendships after she is married, it is also unwise for her single friends to react negatively toward the shift in relationship. A mature friendship will allow for flexibility, and even distance, during the couple's establishment of a marriage friendship. Wait graciously for the reestablishment of your former friendship.

SEEKING FEMALE FRIENDSHIPS

Single women face a constant struggle to have balanced friendships. We become lopsided in our relationships when we seek convenience and safety. Social life should extend beyond your unmarried colleagues at the office or your singles' group at church. Consider your married peers as viable options for friendship. Seek friends who will broaden and extend your horizons. Some of my closest friendships include married peers and their husbands. Some close friends are younger than I am, and others are older. How do we as single women go about establishing appropriate friendships?

Single women are often suspicious of their married peers. In church settings, this breeds feelings of inferiority. Could the lack of bridging-friendships between married and single women be caused primarily by ignorance? The married woman wrongly assumes that the single lady might not want to be part of her world of "wifing" and mothering. The single woman assumes the married woman wouldn't care about her loneliness as a career woman. I have talked to single ladies who felt that married women should initiate the friendships. Why? Single ladies are just as capable of building friendships.

One benefit of seeking a broader range of friendships is balance. My friends who are married keep me grounded in reality. It is easy to assume that marriage would take care of my loneliness, my fears, and my emptiness. Having a close friend who is married shatters such assumptions! Younger friends help me avoid becoming stuffy and old. They keep me current with challenges they face as young people. Your younger friends appreciate the wisdom and comfort your age brings. Seek out older women as well—friends who can mentor you and teach you from their life experiences. Your range and age of friendships will bring quality and substance into your friendship realm.

Seek a broad range of friendship levels as a single lady. It is extremely vital that you do engage at the Accessible Heart Level with a few married and unmarried women. Accountability with a few close friends is healthy and keeps you balanced in a single world. Reject the temptation to use this level exclusively with one single female. Relating primarily to one person narrows your world. We are most vulnerable when relating at this level in our loneliness as single women. The warning signals begin blinking when two single women do everything together. They attend and sit together at the same socials, they go to the same community functions, they take the same vacations, and they function together socially as married people do. Many Christian single women have later regretted the unwholesome relationship that limited them to each other.

SEEKING MALE FRIENDSHIPS

While friendship levels may be somewhat relaxed with our female friends, they must acquire definite boundaries in male friendships. Friendships with men add a whole different dimension to our relational experiences. They produce a different dynamic of their own. As single women, what levels of male friendship should we enter? Can a single lady have a healthy man-friendship without her heart becoming entangled romantically? A woman's emotional hunger seeks continual filling. How can a woman safely engage in male friendships while keeping her heart intact?

For most single women, the Acquaintance Level and Associative Level are safe places from which to engage with single male friends. There is little expectation on either side. The yellow caution light comes on when a male friendship moves into the Affectionate Level. You as a woman have begun giving from your heart a piece of who you are. At this point, if he is married, the red flags go up. If he is single, either you or he must eventually pull back unless you both have interest in pursuing or developing the friendship further; otherwise, it can produce devastating results.

Married couples offer a unique opportunity for friendship. As I said before, some of my closest friends are married couples. Both the husband and wife know me well and contribute meaningfully to my life as a single. I am honored when they invite me along on a family outing or have me over for dinner. Their interaction adds joy and balance to my life as a single.

But again, as single ladies we need to be cautious and not treat such friendships carelessly. Though you are good friends, avoid time alone with the husband. Avoid becoming closer to the husband than the wife. Never should you share personal things with the husband that you will not share with his wife who is your friend. Regard their marital relationship with honor and integrity, and commit yourself to its safekeeping.

Affectionate Level friendships with married couples (outside of family) require a commitment to walk wisely with each other. This level also blinks the yellow caution light, but you must not necessarily pull back. You are given a healthy male-interaction that can offer you balance and perspective.

Any such discussion of male friendships brings us to another big question for single women. How do we know whether we should continue opening our hearts to someone with whom we could potentially have a marriage friendship? How do we know if it is God's will? How long must we wait as single ladies? We will seek answers for such questions in our next chapter.

chapter ten

LADY-IN-WAITING

One day my sister grabbed her children's anecdote notebook when she realized that her young daughter's candid comment might lead to a serious conversation. They had just taken their first bites of lunch when Jaci announced with an air of dramatic expression, "Mommy, I have *two* problems."

"What are they, Jaci?" asked her mother, attempting to stifle a smile.

Exasperated, Jaci proceeded to share that Dalton *liked* her and Lath *loved* her. Dalton and Lath were two boys who attended the same preschool Jaci attended. Jaci's sighs and shaking head added to the comedy of this scenario.

Her mother, barely able to respond seriously, said, "Jaci, I have a solution."

Jaci interrupted questioningly, "Face it?" Before her mother could reply, Jaci added seriously, "Turn the other cheek?" Her mother exploded with laughter. Embarrassed, Jaci looked down.

Quickly gathering her wits, her mother continued, "Jaci, you are friendly and other children like that. It's good that you are friendly." She posed a gentle question. "Why don't you want them to like you and love you?"

"Because they probably want to *doo-dum-de-dum*." She sang the opening line of the traditional "Bridal March." Again Jaci's mother fought to contain her smile.

Jaci added yet another problem. "They're trying to make me like them too," she sighed, and shook her head in despair.

Jaci's mother tried to console her by telling her not to worry about it, and to treat these boys like she treated everyone else. That advice did not satisfy Jaci; she was sure those boys would like her even more. She then came up with her own solution in the midst of her two very serious problems. She would ignore Dalton and Lath and not play with them anymore.

My niece was already discovering the gift of attraction between male and female. How could a preschool child even begin to articulate the tension she felt with the young boys' attraction to her? I believe that God places such desires and attractions in the heart of every male and female. From the beginning of Creation, God intended that men and women would be drawn to each other.

OH, WHERE? OH, WHERE CAN THEY BE?

Kelly's lip trembled as she pulled out her friend's wedding invitation. She loved attending weddings, but would she ever be dressed as a bride? Kelly recalled how she and her friends, in their crazier moments, sang a little ditty, "Oh, where? Oh, where have the good men gone? Oh, where? Oh, where can they be?" The reality of that song never seemed starker than now, as her years increased and her options decreased.

There are times we single ladies have felt the frustration of not being able to capture the man of our dreams. Why do some women have multiple men vying for their attention, while many others do not even have one man casting furtive looks in their direction? Is there something wrong with a single woman who does not attract a man? One thing is certain: availability does not equal attraction.

Women are attracted to men for security and love. A Christian single woman faces a dilemma in her attraction to male relationships. How should she relate to men in ways that keep her heart soft and tender, yet not emotionally entangled? How can she actively hope for the gift of marriage without becoming consumed by that longing? Why does she long for a male counterpart even when one has never been offered?

CANNOT LIVE WITHOUT THEM

Most young women cannot conceive the idea of singlehood. Yet in an imperfect world, singlehood does become a reality for many women. Though we have grown-up hearts, we women are much like Jaci in our super-awareness of men's movement toward us or lack of movement toward us. Panic and fear may grip our hearts in the wake of this knowledge. In a world where male relationships spin out of our control, we determine to come up with our own solutions and strategies to manage them. Single women are tempted to compromise in three ways.

Some focus on comparing their *lack* with others' *luck*, creating fertile ground for a root of bitterness to sprout. Bitterness fosters cynicism and anger, and other people become the target of negative attitudes. Other singles face a subtle temptation to squelch all desire to have a husband. Unfulfilled desire is too painful to embrace. A habitual deadening of desire hardens a woman's heart and destroys her alluring femininity. Finally, the desperate single may be tempted to compromise her virginity. Women in this love-vacuum forfeit integrity for a whisper of gratification.

Being a Christian certainly does not eradicate desire or temptation. Our human tendency is to find quick solutions for our discomforts and dilemmas. However, our "solutions" are usually antithetical to faith and hope. Therefore the woman who tells herself that she doesn't want or need a husband is often simply wearing a survival façade. I am not including in this category victims of abusive situations. Rather, I am speaking to the woman who is negative about marriage because no man has pursued her. In her pain and disappointment, she is rejecting God's original design for a man and woman to become one flesh. She shuts off the natural desire to engage her heart and redirects that energy into a pious commitment of her own making.

We cannot escape the fact that men and women are attracted to each other by God's design. Our internal longing is a God-breathed desire. How then should single women guard their vulnerable femininity in the midst of uncertainty and disappointment? God calls us to become ladies-in-waiting.

LADY-IN-WAITING

During the medieval era, lovely young women were chosen to attend and serve royal ladies. Being chosen as a lady-in-waiting was enviable. Entrance was granted into royal chambers and honorable social events. The lady-in-waiting did not command her mistress; rather, the mistress dictated the life of the lady-in-waiting. Serving in the royal court confined her to the mistress's pace and timing. She could not impede or hasten her mistress's decisions in the matters at hand. She could not seek her own glory or demand the satisfaction of her own needs, but became the recipient of her mistress's grace and goodness. The lady-in-waiting was there for one purpose, and that was to attend and serve the mistress at her bidding.

Godly single women, too, have the high calling to become ladies-in-waiting. We attend and serve no mere human, but the divine Lover of our souls. A single woman is called to entrust her whole life and future to His grace and goodness. She willingly chooses to wait—to "remain in readiness or in anticipation"[1]— for Him to move as He wills. Waiting upon God is not antithetical to desire, but rather is desire embraced. God calls His sons and daughters to wait upon Him and wait for Him.

A woman becomes dismayed when she is forced to wait upon something or someone. She becomes anxious when men don't move toward her. Waiting does not come naturally to us as women. We have an innate compulsion to fix everything right now. We must learn that we cannot hasten God's movement and timing in His men or in His work. Our unbelief or sullen resistance toward His timing impedes the work of God in our hearts. Becoming ladies-in-waiting is a lifetime process. As we wait upon God, He will teach us how to be ladies-in-waiting, His way. In so doing, we are prepared to honor Him and the men He may bring into our lives.

DEPTH AND BREADTH OF MALE RELATIONSHIPS

In our last chapter, we discussed levels of single women's friendships at large. We will now look at these friendship levels again, but this time focus specifically on our friendships with single males. Additionally, we will place a rose legend alongside the friendship levels to signify a woman's heart engagement in the friendship.

ROSE LEGEND	
WHITE ROSE	Signifies no emotional bonding or expectations of a person
YELLOW ROSE	Signifies a casual acquaintance with little expectation
PEACH ROSE	Signifies an established relational interaction formed by default
PINK ROSE	Signifies a warm friendship that has begun to bond emotionally
RED ROSEBUD	Signifies an engaging friendship that has spirit and soul bonds and ties
RED ROSE	Signifies a committed friendship that has spirit, soul, and body bonds and ties

Agape Level: **White Rose**

In this level of friendship, you recognize your link to the broad range of humanity. *Agape* love is not personal friendship, but a God-love demonstrated toward all mankind. *Agape* love looks upon the human race with respect and honor, recognizing people as God's image bearers. Therefore each man you meet is worthy of kindness and compassion. This level, put at the base of any other friendship level, empowers you and the men you meet to be touched by God through a meaningful interchange, however brief or long.

Acquaintance Level: **Yellow Rose**

In *Acquaintance Level* relationships, you are friendly but reserved. You meet these single men occasionally at school, work, social functions, et cetera. Your interchange is strictly general. Your discussions are non-personal and will center on current events, general knowledge, or people connections. In social settings it is respectful for you to graciously acknowledge the presence of these male acquaintances if you chance to meet. But because there is no personal commitment to each other, you as a woman have no obligation to make your presence known to the man if he doesn't initiate it.

Associative Level: **Peach Rose**

The field of males is narrowing at this level. Here you mingle regularly with certain men because of common interests, careers, singles' groups, churches, or institutions. You have established some rapport with these men and you enjoy casual interaction. You may know some personal aspects of each other's lives. Even though your conversations remain mostly at a cognitive level, you find them stimulating and encouraging. No expectations or romantic emotional bonds have formed in either you or him at this point. If the single man would move or disengage totally, it would matter to some degree, but the disappointment would not be acute.

Affectionate Level: **Pink Rose**

This level becomes more serious. You, as a single lady, have now begun a very close interaction with a few single men, which may eventually narrow to one specific man. At this stage, you enjoy bantering camaraderie and soul fellowship with each other. Because you are becoming very good friends, some sharing will happen at a heart level. Although you dare ask more personal questions of each other, there still remains a level of restraint and mystery within this friendship. At this point, one of you may want to take your friendship to a romantic level. Often, unknown to the single man, the single lady has begun forming emotional bonds with him because of his attention and affirmation. Should the man retreat, she would keenly feel the loss of this friendship and find herself grieving for a period of time.

A word of caution: Only very mature single women can operate at the Affectionate Level for a long period of time. It seems that for most single women, the relationship must either mature to the next level or be allowed to regress to a less intense level if the woman is to maintain emotional stability. It is hardly possible for her to sustain a friendship that engages her heart, but does not develop. The woman cannot leave the Affectionate Level without experiencing some repercussions for having engaged in the friendship.

Accessible Heart Level: **Red Rosebud**

Friendship at this level must be limited to a courting relationship with marriage as its end goal. You and a single man share romantic love for each other and express it in respectful and honoring ways. You both are willing to be known at a soul and spirit level, although initially there remains some cautious restraint.

If, for some reason, both of you arrive at the conclusion that marriage is not a viable option, it is critical that the relationship be annulled immediately. If, however, the friendship deepens, at some point in this level both you and the man will commit yourselves to love one another for life. Each of you now reinforces your soul bonds and ties as you share heart secrets and life experiences. Your relationship becomes exclusive. This level is based on trust and commitment. Losing your male friend would be intensely raw and shattering.

Ardent Level: **Red Rose**

Finally, the ardent level is reserved solely for marriage between husband and wife. Ardent love is the most intimate of levels in emotional arousal and attachment. This level brings the capacity to know and be known in one's spirit, soul, and body. The *Ardent Level* is designed to be the highest level of friendship two people can experience. Separation by divorce or death is the literal tearing of the spirit, soul, and body bonds between two soul mates. Loss at this level is the most devastating of all.

Remember that our levels need fluidity to some degree. In the first four levels, friends may move back and forth from one level to another. Each friendship serves its time and purpose. As women, we tend to seek friendships that will create for us some sense of stability and security. It is important that we keep an open hand in the friendships that develop with single men. We should view a male friendship as a gift from God and ask Him to guard our hearts.

Ideally, female and male friendships begin at an acquaintance level and work their way to more intimate levels. These levels should move more slowly than they do in female friendships. Bypassing any one of these levels may have serious implications. If a single woman begins immediately at the Affectionate Level or the Accessible Heart Level, she has violated an integral part of her heart. Unknown to her, she has assimilated into her spirit a level of mistrust concerning this man, who stole a portion of her heart without a commitment to honor her first as an image bearer.

Because of the possibilities of negative emotional bonds and ties, it is dangerous for a single woman to share too much of her heart too soon, or she risks dire consequences. More than one woman has been deeply hurt when what seemed like a budding friendship turned sour. She felt keenly disappointed when the man dropped her for another woman or some other interest.

A SHATTERED HEART

Becky Thatcher, in the book *Tom Sawyer*, is the epitome of a woman with a broken heart. Though only a child, Becky had been wooed by her friend Tom's overt attention and warm affection. Initially, she knew she must be cautious about giving too much of her heart to Tom. Yet by and by she reluctantly assented to his insistence for a vocal declaration of love. She finally whispered timidly, "I–love–you!" After saying those words, she bounded off with Tom chasing her. He caught her, and she helplessly succumbed to Tom's entreaties to kiss her. Then Tom made the blunder of his life.

*"Now it's all done, Becky. And always after this,
you know, you ain't ever to love anybody but me,
and you ain't ever to marry anybody but me, ever
never and forever. Will you?"*

*"No, I'll never love anybody but you, Tom, and I'll
never marry anybody but you—and you ain't to
ever marry anybody but me, either."*

*"Certainly. Of course. That's part of it. And always
coming to school or when we're going home,
you're to walk with me, when there ain't anybody
looking —and you choose me and I choose you at
parties, because that's the way you do when you're
engaged."*

"It's so nice. I never heard of it before."

"Oh, it's ever so gay! Why, me and Amy Lawrence—"

*The big eyes told Tom his blunder and he stopped,
confused.*

*"Oh, Tom! Then I ain't the first you've ever been
engaged to!"*

The child began to cry. Tom said:

"Oh, don't cry, Becky, I don't care for her any more."

"Yes, you do, Tom—you know you do."[2]

Tom tried to make amends, but Becky's heart was shattered.
She ran to the corner of the room, sobbing her heart out. Tom
made a few attempts to remedy his blunder, but Becky rebuffed
his every effort. He finally strutted off, leaving Becky alone in
her tears and despair.

Although we may smile at the childishness of this romance, the scene is eerily profound. Becky had an internal caution flag that made her hesitate to give a portion of her heart to a boy. Yet in her desire to belong to someone special, she threw aside all caution. When she admitted her love and yielded herself to be kissed, she gave her whole heart.

When Tom admitted to having another love, Becky saw through it with amazing clarity. She could not bear the fact that Tom did not give his whole heart to her as she did to him. By giving part of himself to Amy Lawrence, he could give only a part of himself to Becky. Becky felt violated and shamed. She had succumbed naively to the longing to be loved, and it took her heart to the abyss of sorrow.

Tom seemed confused as to why Becky was so devastated. Yet any woman could identify. Becky offered not only her body, but the very core of who she was. Women cannot separate their hearts from their bodies. Men don't always grasp how quickly and deeply women bring their hearts into a relationship.

MORE EXAMPLES OF EMOTIONAL AND RELATIONAL BONDS

Friendships and community are made up of heart bonds and ties. The Apostle Paul encouraged the Ephesians to work at maintaining such bonds within the body of Christ. When I think of bonds and ties, I usually think of ropes. But as Paul used the bond analogy, it did not carry the connotation of a rope. Rather, bonds were something fleshy, warm, and alive. He indicated that these bonds are like joint ties or ligaments (Ephesians 4:3-4, 16). They become the unseen connection between two parts, enabling them to work in harmony with each other in the body of Christ. In any relationship, we cannot physically see the soul bonds and ties, but we can *feel* that there is a connection.

Male and female friendships are built on similar synchronizations of emotional heart bonds and ties. An emotional bond is a warm felt connection with the presence of the man. Thus, a woman opening her heart to romantic feelings needs to be cautious. When a woman moves into male relationship at the Affectionate Level or any higher level, she brings her heart. In this she will be tempted to romanticize the relationship, fantasizing not necessarily about the man's body, but his protection, kindness, and love. She begins dreaming of all he could be for her, and of the security and intimacy his love would provide.

A woman will tend to open her heart to a man when he begins listening to her at a heart level. As he listens, she shares more; the more she shares, the more of her heart she gives. This is why cross-gender counseling has its limitations. Occasionally, a single or married woman will seek a male counselor to simulate a relationship she longs to have and cannot get any other way. She will give her heart to the counselor, who is gentle and understanding in a safe, affirming environment. Such emotional bonds and ties have negative implications in the woman's future relationships. They create unrealistic expectations for any other male relationship the woman will have.

It is possible to create an emotional bond with any man even with limited interaction. A woman can meet a man one time and let her mind run wild with imagination of how this man might move toward her with strength and protection. In giving her heart, she also creates an emotional bond with the man. Her level of emotional oneness with him causes her to feel an equal level of feminine wholeness.

Emotional bonds and ties are not wrong when operating within appropriate commitments. Rather, they are God-given. But outside of commitment, they have distressing implications. When moving closer in relationship with a man, a woman must constantly ask herself, "Is he pursuing me for a commitment, or is he just enjoying my friendship?" Discover the intentions of the man before you give too much of your heart and soul.

If a woman has shared the Affectionate Level or Accessible Heart Level with a man, but the relationship has dissolved, it is extremely crucial that she break the resulting emotional bonds. Failure to sever her heart connections with him will inhibit her freedom to love another man in the future with the same capacity.

A woman offering any part of her body to a man experiences more than physical connection. It creates warm feelings that stem from her need for love. She will offer him her body to receive his heart. With her body she brings along all her emotions surrounding the man. She cannot separate the physical and the emotional experience into separate entities.

When she experiences sexual intimacy it is no different. Author Paula Rinehart says, "Your heart and soul will follow your body."[3] At this point a woman creates a tie that can be broken only by a tearing of the woman's emotions and heart. Rinehart further suggests, "If a connection to a man is made and broken—made and broken again and again—you may lose your capacity to bond to someone deeply. Like glue that has been squeezed out of a tube, everything inside has been spent and you feel numb."[4] Eventually the woman becomes a shell of existence.

That is why sexual intimacy outside of marriage is so devastating and scarring.

What are the warning flags for single women who wonder if they have crossed the line with emotional and relational bonds? The book *Every Woman's Battle* suggests a list of questions that a woman may ask herself in determining her level of emotional bonding.

* Do you think of this man often (several times each day) even though he is not around?
* Do you select your daily attire based on whether you will see this person?
* Do you go out of your way to run into him, hoping he'll notice you?
* Do you look for excuses to call him so you can hear his voice?
* Do you find reasons to e-mail him, eagerly anticipating his response?
* Do you wonder if he feels any attraction toward you?
* Do you want to talk or spend time alone with this person, out of earshot or eyesight of anyone else?[5]

How does a woman break free from the entanglements of inappropriate emotional or relational bonding? I cannot list a step-by-step process, but will offer some things that I feel are key elements in gaining freedom. First, a woman must recognize the inappropriate emotional bonds that have been formed, hindering her freedom in relating to others. She must make a conscious choice to let them go, releasing her demand that the relationship work for her ends. And she must turn her whole heart to the One who can free her!

She may find it helpful to pray aloud that she chooses to release this emotional or heart bond with _____ (naming the person), and that she gives God permission to sever it. Something can happen in the speaking that may not happen when we only think the thoughts. A woman also may find it more helpful to ask a trusted friend to pray with her for deliverance and healing from the trap of unhealthy bonds than to pray alone.

Emotional and heart bonds are born out of a desire for connection. God calls a lady-in-waiting to reserve her heart for Him and the man He will bring to her in His time.

HOW LONG MUST I WAIT?

The big question in a single lady's mind (to a greater or lesser degree) is, "Will I *ever* get married?" This question floats in and out of her thoughts, whether she is twelve, twenty, forty, sixty, or even older. She might wonder, "What does it take to get a husband? How long must I wait?" Maybe you will agree with Annemarie in the excerpt below, as she is interviewed by the author of *Heart to Heart about Men: Words of Encouragement for Women of Integrity.*

> Annemarie and I sat across from each other in the half-empty restaurant and talked over breakfast. She was twenty-one, the daughter of dear friends, and I had a few questions I wanted to ask her.
>
> "What do you think a woman most longs to receive from a man?" I began.

After a thoughtful pause, she replied with a firm nod, "His heart."

"And what do you think a man most longs to give to a woman?" I also wanted to know.

"Not his heart," she answered without hesitation.

"Why not?" I pursued.

"Because he knows if he gives his heart he's done for. He can't take it back." [6]

Annemarie's insight powerfully illustrates what nearly every woman knows. If she can captivate and capture a man's heart, her quest is over.

WOMAN-OF-THE-WORLD: SEDUCTIVE POWER

The desire for love incites women to devise ways (consciously and unconsciously) of capturing men's hearts. When we read the description of a seductive woman in Proverbs, we recognize a familiar worldly icon in American culture. We see her alluring beauty on magazines, billboards, and movies. A woman's physical beauty is her trump card in turning a man's head and captivating his heart. Worldly women seduce men with coy eyes, flattering speech, and dolled-up bodies. A man who lacks integrity and truth will be easy prey in her ploy to capture his heart.

Eyes are a powerful medium to connect two hearts. The old adage, "Eyes are the windows to the soul," is never more true than when a male and female connect in this way. The worldly woman's desire for a man overrides any shred of modesty in communicating with her eyes. She invites him to notice her flirtatious sweeping lashes. Other times, with bold, saucy eyes, she holds the gaze of a man, daring him to respond to her invitation. A man's innate desire to conquer is challenged when a woman blatantly dares him to initiate movement. Seductive communication with her eyes creates immediate intimacy, and bypasses the appropriate growth of friendship levels.

The wellspring of a woman's heart is revealed by her lips and her words. During intimate conversations, the seductive woman employs her soft, alluring voice to quicken his manliness. The Proverbs writer depicted the power of a worldly woman's words. He wrote: "For the lips of an immoral woman drip honey, and her mouth is smoother than oil" (Proverbs 5:3). Again in Proverbs 7:21 we read, "With her enticing speech she caused him to yield, with her flattering lips she seduced him." Such a woman uses enthralling speech to lure the man. He is caught off balance when she offers him her soft lips.

Any woman knows that even more powerful than her eyes or mouth is her physical body. Worldly women will flaunt their bodies with seductive clothing that leaves a man goggle-eyed and drunk with the memory. A woman's clothing and body movements powerfully impact a man. If a man is drawn to such a woman, most often his intentions are for immediate pleasure and gratification. He may walk away empowered as a man, but careless or unaware of the shattering effects on the woman and the downward spiral of his own soul.

In the deepest recesses of every woman's heart there is an intense longing to be loved and protected. The worldly woman's desperation for completion and connection allows her to compromise virtuous femininity by using physical avenues to seduce men. Unfortunately, she discovers too late the deadly repercussions of her seduction. Men become conquerors of her body instead of protectors.

Eric Ludy suggests that in every male is a warrior heart. He writes, "A warrior is more than just a defender of truth and justice and a champion for the weak. A warrior is also trained to protect what is sacred and innocent within a woman."[7] When the warrior ignores the sacred nature of femininity, it leads to devastating results for both the woman and the man.

LADY-IN-WAITING: SOFTNESS POWER

Popular culture mocks the woman who retains her virginity and purity and calls her archaic and Victorian. Virtuous single women are not shamed by such labels. Godly women find it difficult to compete against the worldly-wise women in actions and lifestyle, but neither do they need or want to compete. Their sights reach far beyond the desire for momentary pleasure. Godly women turn their eyes, voices, and bodies toward an eternal kingdom, and render their gifts for its cause. Their King teaches them to rely on Him, rest in Him, and reserve themselves for Him.

A lady-in-waiting who relies on God also trusts in Him. Her eyes are turned toward Him. She can then turn her eyes outward in honest reflection, being filled with the graciousness of God's Spirit. A lady-in-waiting does not feel the desperate compulsion to flirt to attract a male, but rather invites godly relationship with warm, kind eyes. She uses her eyes to reflect respect and honor toward men, who are God's image bearers. Her eyes do not dare a man, but rather yield with deference. Her eyes do not roll in disgust and degradation, but open wide with delight. Her eyes do not slit in anger, but glisten with tears. She allows her eyes to become the windows of truth that call men to respond to her in honoring ways.

Resting in God's timing is a challenge for any woman. This is especially true in relation to the men in her life. After Ruth went to Boaz during the night, she did not know how the matter would be resolved. Her mother-in-law then asked her to do a very difficult thing. She said, "'Sit still, my daughter, until you know how the matter will turn out'" (Ruth 3:18). Can you imagine how disconcerting this was for Ruth? In her era before cell phoning and texting, she had no way to keep current with Boaz concerning the proceedings at the gate. How did she manage?

Remember this—saying everything you know, think, and understand is stripping the power and beauty of feminine mystique.

In our technological world, we have lost the gift of distance. Courting has a vastly different form today than it did in my parents' era of the fifties. My mother and father would see each other only on weekends. They occasionally called each other or sent snail mail, but their communication was very limited. There was much my parents did not know about each other when they married.

Today with e-mail and cell phones, we can bridge distance with a few quick punches on a keypad. Unfortunately, in this new era women have also lost the beauty of mystery. A woman's compulsion to share with a man everything (or most things) about herself is detrimental to that God-given sense of mystery. A godly woman will speak, but she will do so with discretion and wisdom, resting in the fact that she need not say everything she knows. Her words will be gentle and kind. According to 1 Peter

3:1, a woman makes the most impact when she chooses her words carefully and appropriately. When a woman has a compulsion to be speaking all the time, she struggles to be a woman at rest.

A godly lady-in-waiting offers not only her eyes of trust and her words of wisdom, but also her body as an instrument of righteousness. This does not mean that she needs to wear dowdy or shabby clothes to be righteous. I believe quite the opposite is true.

Sometimes in Christian circles a woman's desire for beauty is squelched. We fear beauty because we understand its raw power to entice. Yet God created woman beautiful in both spirit and body. When His loveliness is radiating from her heart, it causes external effects. The direction is crucial. She does not look to outward beauty as the gateway to inner joy; rather, His inward beauty revolutionizes the outward. The focus then is not on the senses but on the life within. A woman becomes appealing in the right sense, free to give outward expression of Christ's beauty within her life.

Cleanliness, muscle tone, modesty, and moderation all accent the beauty and glory of femininity. Add virginity to that, and you see a godly woman who is protecting her body—for the man who may someday be her husband, and certainly for Jesus Christ. She becomes a lady of grace and dignity. Such a woman is rare and starkly in contrast to worldly standards, but her price exceeds that of rubies! (Proverbs 31:10).

STILL WONDERING—WILL I EVER GET MARRIED?

The question of whether or not you will get married was not answered in this chapter, and the answer may be long in coming.

Yes, you have learned about holding your heart carefully in male friendships. You have discovered the secret strengths of a lady-in-waiting. Yet you are still waiting.

Much of life requires waiting. Your waiting is a process. The process is not a linear path that will automatically lead you to a husband. A precise following of steps and strategies will not promise you the results you seek. Certainly, doing everything "right" does not ensure a dream fulfilled. Rather, the process opens your heart toward eternal values and eternal goals.

God asks us to wait for Him. Waiting upon God bends our hearts toward Him. In the bending, we deepen our understanding. In the bending and deepening, we begin seeing a larger picture of His purposes and His goodness. This allows us to become deeply acquainted with God's ways and not just His acts. Ultimately, waiting brings us to the heart of the Father; there we find rest.

Today my mother cut a delicate pink peony from her cluster to put in a vase on my desk. It is my own. This lone flower has been sitting on my desk, in all its loveliness and fragrance, for the duration of the afternoon. Did it choose to sit solitary on my desk? No. It is here strictly for my purposes and enjoyment. Are you getting the picture?

God's purposes are beyond our understanding and choosing. Can I keep my eyes, mouth, and body pure to serve God's purpose in this generation?

Will God bring me a husband? Maybe He will and maybe He won't. Does the knowing matter? Not truly. What *does* matter? It matters that I submit to God and to His plan, which is larger than I understand. I am here on this earth for God's purpose and glory, and that is answer enough.

chapter eleven

THE HEART AT HOME

In my early forties, I relocated from Indiana to northwestern Pennsylvania one warm August morning. A few of my family members assisted me by traveling along and unpacking boxes in my spacious two-bedroom apartment. The next day I squeezed back the tears and swallowed a lump in my throat as I waved good-bye. I felt like a fledgling in this life-changing transition to a new community and teaching job.

I slowly walked into my apartment. I was alone for the first time in my life. However, before the end of the following week, I opened my home to another single female teacher. Patty and I shared that living arrangement until her marriage, three years later.

I had lived in Indiana for most of my life, and boarded at my parents' home as an adult. My parents were pro-education; therefore, they graciously subsidized my modest wages at the local private school by providing low housing costs for me. To help compensate for their generosity, I assisted them with the domestic duties of running a household. Even with this living arrangement at its best, I knew that at some point in my life I would need to have my own home. Now the time had come.

Being responsible for an apartment gave me a greater taste of independence. Patty and I soon became friends. We were not dependent on each other, yet our arrangement certainly required flexibility for us. We each tried to respect the other's needs, preferences, and idiosyncrasies. Living together was a positive experience for both of us because we valued our friendship and our living arrangement.

When Patty married, I keenly missed her presence. I found the silence had a sound of its own. There were no doors slamming, no footsteps pattering, and no cheery greetings. I had not realized how much presence and companionship just one person brought into a home. I became acutely aware of my aloneness as a single. At that time, God set me on a journey that taught me how I could experience unmitigated connection and completion with Christ regardless of my marital status. He gave my heart a home, and I found a place to belong. This is the journey I now share with you.

"YOU ARE A BIG GIRL NOW"

While going through college years ago, I picked up a waitressing job at a local restaurant. One day I chatted with two couples at a table. During our brief interchange one of the men asked whether I had my own home. In my naïveté, I replied that I lived with my parents. Smirking, he informed me that I was a big girl now and should be living on my own. He thought it ridiculous that my living arrangement included my parents. As I saw it, that arrangement was one of God's precious gifts to me.

How long should single ladies live with their parents? There are no easy answers. Sometimes life events provide a natural breaking point. Some ladies move away from home in order to attend college. For others, a career may necessitate finding their own living quarters. Some women move out as an escape from relational tensions.

Other single women have no definitive marker, no "reason" to cause the establishment of a home. Suppose marriage does not come for the single woman by the time she is thirty, forty, or fifty? How should she determine the timing of moving out of her parents' home and establishing her own home?

No matter where a woman finds herself, I do believe it is crucial for her to find a home. To me, "home" means her sanctuary—her place of refuge, belonging, and delight. For a single lady, the goal of finding her own home should not be wrapped up in a selfish desire for independence. Rather, the goal of a home is to give godly expression to the single woman's identity and calling.

"RETURN HOME, WOMAN"

Hagar, a single woman, encountered a stressful relationship with her mistress, Sarai, and fled into the wilderness to make her home. Unfortunately, there was no sanctuary in that barren land. Threat of wild animals, lack of vegetation, and limited water supply forced Hagar to face some harsh realities. Pregnant and depleted, Hagar wandered beneath the blazing sun. She wiped her eyes and screamed back into the howling wilderness, "I don't have to take all that harsh treatment from Sarai! I don't! I don't!" Sweat dripped from her face and mingled with her tears as she trudged through the pathless sea of sand.

TO HAVE AND TO HOLD

To her amazement, she stumbled onto a little oasis. A spring bubbled generously from the ground. Finding water in the wilderness was amazing enough, but even more astounding was the fact that God drew near to meet her. A messenger of the Lord instructed Hagar to change her course of action and return to the home and family she knew. She would birth her child in Sarai's tent.

Her awed comment was, "You-Are-the-God-Who-Sees... 'Have I also here seen Him who sees me?'" (Genesis 16:13). God saw this single, pregnant woman plodding along in the wilderness. Although she had sinned against her mistress by despising her, God did not reject Hagar. He cared enough to aid her with provision and protection. He commanded her to return to her former family and accept the support she needed from them.

"Well, that was Hagar," you might say, "but does God still meet single women in their wildernesses today?"

This morning during my quiet time, I read the account in Luke in which Jesus reminded His disciples that the God of the universe notices the insignificant sparrow that flutters and twitters upon this earth. "'Are not five sparrows sold for two copper coins? And not one of them is forgotten before God...Do not fear therefore; you are of more value than many sparrows'" (Luke 12:6-7).

Every individual upon this earth is infinitely precious in God's sight. I would like to think that when any woman finds herself in helpless, hopeless, and distressing situations, God's heart is greatly moved with compassion. He sees her vulnerability. In those moments He leans down from His habitation and works on her behalf. Yes, that even includes the single woman, who, like Hagar, yearns for a place to belong and find her heart at home.

GOD SETS THE SOLITARY

The Psalmist describes a few groups of people that draw God's particular attention. God sees these people from His holy habitation. The Psalmist emphasizes that God not only notices, but moves on behalf of these specific groups, as "a father of the fatherless, a defender of widows…God sets the solitary in families; He brings out those who are bound" (Psalm 68:5-6).

God provides solutions for those in need. When He reaches out to the fatherless, He becomes a Father to them. He tells the widows that He will become their Advocate. Now, both the widows and fatherless may already have learned dependency through existing supportive relationships. The fatherless often have mothers. Widows most often have families. In their distress, God now calls them to turn from horizontal relationships to a vertical relationship that places their trust and faith in Him.

As we read verse six, we find that for the single people, God does something totally different than He did for the fatherless and widows. It says that He "sets the solitary in families." He puts those who are alone into the context of community. Their need is not *just* for a vertical relationship; they also need the balance of human connection. I believe that is why God sent Hagar back to a family unit.

Single people haven't necessarily encountered the tragedies that surround the fatherless and widows; therefore, their needs may be different. Singles need the encouragement of a small group of people to whom they can belong. Singles' tendency toward independence requires the balance of interdependency. Mingling with other people keeps us grounded in the realities of life and provides community accountability and connection.

MY HOME, MY REST

In ancient cultures, single women and widows rarely lived alone. They needed the stability and protection that parental homes could provide. As we observed earlier in the biblical account, Naomi understood this. She and her daughters-in-law were walking away from a home they had known and loved. Naomi stopped and insisted that these widows return to their former homes and find refuge from their dire circumstances. She urged them to pursue marriage and a place of rest.

Although Orpah returned to her homeland, Ruth clung tenaciously to Naomi's faith and Naomi's God. Naomi allowed Ruth to remain her daughter and companion. Yet even after living together in Israel for a number of months, Naomi still staunchly believed it necessary for Ruth to have her own home. She said, "My daughter, shall I not seek rest for thee, that it may be well with thee?" (Ruth 3:1 KJV). Ruth willingly complied with Naomi's instruction to meet Boaz at the threshing floor. Enchanted with this virtuous young lady, Boaz took action and met with the elders at the gate. In the end, he took Ruth to wife, and her heart found a home among a foreign people in a strange land.

I don't think this story insinuates that for a woman to be at rest, she must find a husband and a home of her own. Nor does Psalm 68:6 mean that a single woman will be unfailingly matched up with a family for the rest of her life. Rather, these passages remind us that our focus must be on yielding to God's idea of rest for single people. He wills that single people find their place among others. Could it be that if a single woman turns her heart toward the Father, He would be delighted to provide small communities for her at various junctures in her life?

We as single women need balance, and we need help. Though our situation would naturally push us toward independence, we simply do not have what it takes to stand alone. We need interaction with the logic and rationality of men. We also need the assistance of their physical strength. We need the emotional bonding of friendships with women. We need an outlet to nurture children. In short, we need the interaction of families. Single women are never more feminine than when they embrace this truth of interdependency and accountability.

CAN ONE BE A FAMILY?

You may be questioning all this talk about belonging to a family. Can *one* not be a family? I suppose the answer depends upon our definition of family. We certainly were created to live in context of connection. Connection cannot go solo; neither can it happen in a vacuum. Without a person-to-person relationship, one hardly has the right to be called a family.

Unfortunately, our postmodern culture has embraced twisted definitions of family. Family lines and responsibilities have become muddied and blurred. God's commandment for a one-man, one-woman marriage has been ignored. Divorce and remarriage break and blend families in ways that were never intended to be. Same-sex partners adopt children and rear them in imitation of a family unit. People have made families into something God never designed.

What is a family, then? Simply explained, God's original idea of family included one man and one woman committed to each other for life. Along with their children, they would work, eat, sleep, and live together. God intended that *family* would provide identity and belonging for each individual and bring each heart to rest.

Can a single lady have a partial family? Could she not adopt children and trust God as her husband? There are many factors one must take into consideration here. One obvious factor is that babies grow up. It is one thing to take care of babies, and quite another to work through adolescent issues and teenage challenges as a single parent. Raising children requires selflessness and much wisdom. A single parent has to carry the weight of both the male and female in parenting children. At its best, such an arrangement remains inadequate and requires a greater measure of maturity.

We read of women such as Gladys Aylward, Amy Carmichael, and Mary Slessor who literally took dozens of children into their homes and raised them without husbands. Certainly if God leads you in that direction, His grace will empower you. Yet if you consider adoption as a single parent, do so carefully and cautiously. If your purpose for adopting children is primarily to fill a void in your life, you would be unwise to pursue it.

In her book *Did I Kiss Marriage Goodbye?*, Carolyn McCulley provides an excellent list of questions for a single lady considering adoption. They range from searching heart motives to carefully considering financial responsibility. The list also includes thinking about your emotional stability, your parenting style, and your possibility of future marriage.[1]

CAN ONE HAVE A HOME?

There is no one right way to build or create a home. Homes are as varied as the materials from which they are constructed. Women have lived in makeshift tents, in cardboard shacks, in mud huts, in modular frames, in ranch-style homes, in stately mansions, and in everything in between. Nearly every woman, at some point in her life, desires to be the mistress of a domain specifically regarded as her territory. Perhaps a woman feels most free to express her femininity and womanhood when her house becomes her home.

Can a single woman have a home? The answer is a resounding "yes!" Even though it takes more than one to make a family, it only takes one to make a home! You do not need to have a husband or children in order to make your house into more than a mere dwelling place.

Some years ago I signed up for a class entitled "The Art of Homemaking," taught by my friend Cynthia. I chose that class for two reasons. First, I wanted to broaden my understanding of my married friends' world of homemaking. Second, I wondered how the art of homemaking might look for a single woman.

I was unprepared for the emotional wave that hit me that first morning as each student shared her reason for signing up for this class. One after the other, the married ladies expressed their need to learn homemaking in the context of their families and husbands. I shared my need to learn homemaking in the lack of a family and husband. I could not hide my tears. In that moment, I was not sure I truly could make a home without a husband and children. I was in for a surprise!

Cynthia's class revolutionized my ideas of homemaking. For the first forty years of my life, I had lived in the context of a family. Family and home seemed synonymous. When I moved to Pennsylvania, I kept busy. I had many career obligations and social engagements. My job as a teacher and mentor demanded much of my time and gave me an identity as a career woman. A homemaker I was not. My apartment was just a house. It certainly did not reflect me as a homemaker.

I often stepped into my apartment as if it were a convenience store or a motel. I dropped by to read my mail, eat, and sleep. I did not see my apartment as a home, but rather as a place to stay when nothing else demanded my attention. After taking the class, I began to realize how limited my perspective on homemaking had been. How does a single lady embrace homemaking in the midst of her career demands? For the remainder of this chapter we will focus on housekeeping and homemaking.

UNLESS THE LORD BUILDS THE HOUSE

Let's return to the questions we raised earlier: How should a single woman determine where to live and what home to have? Ancient Jewish custom stated that a daughter was her father's responsibility until her marriage or her demise. She did not have to fend for herself. Today, the cultural expectations are different. We have moved from an agrarian lifestyle to a technological world. Does that make a difference? Probably it does. With all the modern conveniences, a woman finds it easier to live alone. Scripture is rather silent on this subject. Certainly God's Word does not negate the option of a woman purchasing her own house and making it her home. In fact, it is indicative of a virtuous woman to buy and sell and to manage her possessions wisely, according to Proverbs 31. The Proverbs writer also makes the observation that "the wise woman builds her house, but the foolish pulls it down with her hands" (14:1). A woman is a woman, whether she is married or single; she has the capacity for wisdom and for foolishness. The Hebrew word for *house*[2] denotes the actual structure but could include its interior as well. In this context, the verse suggests that it is perfectly right and good for a woman to seek a place she can call her home.

The late Edith Schaeffer, who wrote *What Is a Family?*, firmly insisted that *L'Abri* was not a commune, but a complex of shared homes. She emphasized the privacy of these homes. There may have been several families living in the same building, but each family had its own living quarters offering privacy to the children and parents. The Schaeffers also believed that each child should have his or her own room and each family should have its own basic possessions. The privacy expectations included singles too. Edith Shaeffer wrote:

> *We believe strongly that single people in L'Abri as Workers ought to have their own apartments or little houses when possible, and that these homes are theirs to share. We very firmly believe that each family should feel that the chalet or apartment or*

house which is its home is really its own in every
way possible.[3]

Mrs. Schaeffer recognized that single women need their own homes as much as families do. She also encouraged singles not to hold their homes selfishly, but to swing the doors open to bless others in the community.

As a general rule, it does not work well for two women to have an equal amount of ownership in a house. A woman's desire to have her own domain causes tension when two women are vying for the same territory. Each senses a need for an expression of herself in her home. In trying to share the ownership of that expression, each becomes a threat to the other's identity. Fairness is not so quickly an issue when one of the two holds the greater portion of ownership and responsibility.

When should a single woman consider buying a house instead of renting or living with her family? This is a question that each woman must answer for herself. Many single women are reluctant to purchase a home, but for varied reasons. A single woman may be hesitant to assume the responsibilities that encumber home-owners, and choose not to purchase a home for that reason. Her preference for freedom and mobility overrides the desire to own a home, and she is perfectly comfortable living with her parents or renting a house.

Another reason may be the ambivalence of an unknown future. A woman may wrongly assume that buying a house expresses her preference for singlehood and hinders her future chances of marriage. But buying a house does not obliterate the opportunity for marriage. She will just have that much more to bring into the marriage when she pools resources with her husband!

However, you can make a home for yourself whether you live with your parents, rent, or buy. If you are vacillating among the options, make it a matter of prayer. God has a vested interest in building your home. Your residence is a place where His glory may be revealed and celebrated. He wants us to look to Him even in matters of housing, according to Psalm 127:1. "Unless the LORD builds the house, they labor in vain who build it." God wants to participate in your efforts. Whether you decide to rent or buy, allow God to build your house, and embrace the gift of homemaking alongside your career or job.

DEATHS TO A DREAM

I often wondered what the future would hold for me in relation to housing. I am a teacher of moderate means, and swinging the cost of purchasing a home seemed an unlikely possibility. In fact, if I focused on my income, it was an impossible dream. At times people would ask me if I would like to purchase a home. I would look at them bleakly and think, "If you knew my limited finances, you wouldn't ask!"

I am amazed at how God works despite our limited faith and resources. In my situation, God used other people to dream what I could not bring myself to dream. I worked under a principal who recognized my need to get away from renting an apartment on school campus. He believed it would be possible for me to invest in some property.

A few years ago on a wintry day he asked me whether I would be interested in buying a house. Of course I would! Hopelessly

I squeaked out, "I would love to own my own home, but I don't have the financial resources."

Mr. Miller smiled and replied, "I don't think that will be a problem. There are financial institutions and lenders that could work with your limited income." He proceeded to tell me of a local duplex that was for sale. It was less than half a mile from the school. I tingled with excitement at the thought of owning a home.

I took trusted friends along to check out the duplex, which was reasonably priced. It was more house than I needed, but it had possibilities. I could easily rent out one part and live in the other. In fact, the back could be transformed into a third apartment. Sure, the house needed some work, but I was optimistic.

I made copies of the information and called my family. But their response was negative. One brother told me, "Sharon, it would take a lot to fix up the place, and besides, you are not rental property material." I felt a squeeze of disappointment, but I knew what he said was true. I am not mechanically inclined. I would have to hire workmen for everything that needed to be done. I also would never have the heart to charge rent to anyone in a financial crisis.

I kept waiting and hoping for the right house. The following winter, another possibility surfaced. This was a newly renovated home, though the interior was still unfinished. Again I contacted my family. They were not opposed to my buying it, but still thought it was a hefty sum for my limited income. Time elapsed, and in the end the owner decided not to sell. I now faced the second death to my dream.

The third winter finally told a different story. A one-bedroom house was for sale. Everything seemed right—including the price, the location, and the structure. This time each member of my family gave me full support and blessing. At last I moved into the cute white house that has become my home.

Twice the dream of owning a house died, but the fulfillment of the dream came in God's own time. Often we as single women are called to wait upon God to the same degree our married friends need to wait for their husbands' direction. Both routes develop trust and faith. The week I moved into my house, the rose of Sharon tree on my new property was in full bloom. I was awed. It was as though the Lord rejoiced and celebrated with me that my heart had found a home.

BY WISDOM, BY UNDERSTANDING, BY KNOWLEDGE

Your home should reflect you! Women vary in their interests and styles. Deb, my sister just younger than I, has a balance of country and dainty in her home. She paints pastel walls, hangs lacy curtains, and puts up knickknack shelves. She prefers the comforting feel of country with a delicate touch of femininity. My youngest sister, Esther, is drawn to simple and antique items along with splashes of modern décor. She uses words and verses as accents in her rooms. Judy, a friend of mine, appreciates the beauty of flowers. She has a large floral arrangement in each of the main rooms of her house, including flower garlands on a swag curtain or a shelf. Another of my friends has painted the walls of her home in rich neutral colors. Her rooms are highlighted with earth-tone floral arrangements and lush green ferns.

These women have explored their creativity and tastes. They

have dared to make their homes into places that reflect their interests and styles. Do not mimic something that is not you. Your home does not have to look like your best friend's home. It does not matter whether or not others like it. God created you uniquely. If *you* enjoy it with Him, that is what matters.

Consider whether you prefer an elegant, modern, casual, or simple look. Maybe you gravitate toward themes. Are you drawn to themes of nature, ocean, southwestern, or colonial? Maybe your house displays art prints, books, and crafts. Be creative, and enjoy exploring the possibilities!

Some women lament, "But I am not creative. I don't know who I am." Begin by having an opinion about what you like or do not like in a home. Take special note of the various homes you enter, and begin to form your tastes in interior design. As Christian women, we have yet another way to learn. We have the Holy Spirit who is our Teacher and Counselor. We honor God when we open our hearts and minds to His Spirit as we design our homes.

One morning soon after I had moved into my house, I came across a wonderfully exciting passage in Proverbs 24:3-4. "Through wisdom a house is built, and by understanding it is established; by knowledge the rooms are filled with all precious and pleasant riches." Herein lay the answer!

The Holy Spirit began to teach me how to fill my rooms. It was quite cost effective too! I began finding treasures in my own house and in other surprising places with which to accent my home. Now when friends step into my home and say, "Sharon, this is so you!" I smile. God knew what my home needed to reflect something about my femininity and womanhood that would glorify Him.

HOMEMAKING WITHOUT A FAMILY

As a single person, you likely hold a job. Many mothers look enviously at "all that free time" you have. And as a general rule, if you are in your twenties, you do have more free time. You are not yet required to carry the weight of responsibility you may bear in your upper thirties. Yet as an older single woman, you may (with many others) begin lamenting your limited amount of free time. By then, not only will you have become an employee with more responsibility, but you also face a greater load in managing your household and assisting with church and community efforts.

Most single women hold a full-time job that requires anywhere from forty to fifty hours each week. Imagine an eight-hour chunk out of the day and a three-hour evening commitment or social. That wraps up eleven hours of what I call "hard time." This leaves approximately three to four hours of free time in a day. Often, for a single woman, some of the free time is designated to household duties. There are dishes to wash, floors to sweep, trashcans to empty, laundry to fold, and a lawn to mow. While we do not have children to care for, we also do not have a husband to share any part of the workload and responsibility.

How does a working, single woman go beyond basic housekeeping to real homemaking? I agree with my friend Cynthia, who said, "Every single woman can have a home of warmth and delight by looking at two facets of homemaking. These facets are creating a refuge and sharing your refuge." Yes, homemaking will look a bit different for single women than for married women, but the purpose of homemaking will be the same. A home should be a place for living and a place for loving.

HOME, A PLACE TO LIVE

We all need a place to belong; we need a place we can call home. One's home should not be thought of as a mere roof-and-four-walls for existence and shelter, or as a hasty pit stop in the rat race. Rather we need a place that will help us develop and flourish as single women.

For Rest

On a daily basis, a single woman needs to get up and face a world beyond her home. Her job demands a level of physical and emotional stamina. She rubs shoulders with an unfriendly world, requiring her to stay strong and committed if she is going to survive emotionally, physically, and spiritually. Amid the hubbub of the work force, a woman needs a place where she can find refuge from the demands of the public sphere.

When you step inside your door after a day's work, the warmth of hope and comfort should greet you. It can be depressing to step into a cold, dark, messy house. What draws you to your home after work? The key is preparation! Give yourself a few extra minutes in the morning to pick up your clothes, clear your counter, or put something into the crock-pot before you leave for work. You could set out a fresh bouquet that will greet you at the kitchen table. (Local supermarkets often sell lovely floral arrangements for just a few dollars.) Perhaps you could light a small lamp and lay a few books beside it. Try something as simple as telling yourself, "Welcome home!" when you step inside the door.

Think of your home as a place of rest. Rest is the absence of turmoil. Rest radiates peace and brings comfort to your heart and your surroundings. You as a homemaker should create an aura of restfulness in your home that annihilates the demands, fears, and stresses of your day. Pray daily and ask for God's peace to be upon your home. When our hearts are at rest, we will hear God in the silence of our homes, and joy will come.

For Refreshment

Creating rest may sound like an easy, passive approach. But it is not enough. You will also need the gift of refreshment. Your renewed energy will enable you to work with purpose on subsequent days and offer to others something of yourself.

As a homemaker, think of creative ways to refresh the one who does live in your home. That is you! It could mean taking an hour to read something stimulating. Maybe it is putting your feet into a tub of warm water and doing a foot scrub, or taking a pleasant bubble bath. Music always changes perspective. Play a favorite CD that turns your focus to worship and celebration of God's goodness. Your rejuvenation might include nature walks, playing with animals, or going for a bike ride. Maybe all you need for refreshment is sipping a cup of cappuccino in your favorite chair.

We can hardly address refreshment without including food. Make your dinner table inviting for yourself. Take time to light a candle, or use a placemat, or set a crystal goblet, or lay a flower in front of you. When you are eating alone, consider turning on soft music. (Perhaps after a hectic day, you prefer silence, which provides a refreshment all its own.) Eat balanced meals and treat yourself occasionally to a warm cookie. Food is more enjoyable when it is shared with another person. Use holy imagination and ask Jesus to join you for the evening meal. This is your home, and you are the homemaker with unlimited possibilities for creating a place of refreshment.

HOME, A PLACE TO LOVE AND SERVE

So far we have focused on providing rest and refreshment for the in-house resident. Yet our homemaking should not be limited to our own needs and fulfillment. Our energies should also be directed to filling our homes with extensions of love. Immediately you might think, "Who is there to love?" Remember how Isaiah 54 spoke to the childless woman who was to stretch the parameters of her tent? Hospitality was part of the package! She needed to prepare for the crowd coming to her tent.

Hospitality is opening your heart and home to love and serve people through encouragement. Rachael Crabb has given serious thought to the virtue of hospitality. In her book *The Personal Touch: Encouraging Others Through Hospitality*, she writes:

> You are showing your personal involvement by offering hospitality. It is important to remember that [it] has less to do with what you do together than with whether you demonstrate a caring, others-centered attitude that reflects itself in your interaction.[4]

People are delighted to enter our homes when we offer

them refreshment, rest, and love. There are unlimited possibilities. Have the neighbors over for popcorn. Delight your female friends with a tea party. Make some children happy by serving hot dogs and ice cream and then playing a few games with them. Consider hosting out-of-town guests for the weekend. Invite a family for a meal and enjoy a few hours of fun. Food does not always need to be a factor. I have had evenings in which I simply invited a friend over for some chat time. A glass of ice water or a cup of tea sufficed.

I recall the first time I single-handedly attempted to entertain some guests for a formal meal. I worked hard to prepare my food beforehand, but there were still last minute things to do. I had to do a quick food-check before I answered the knock on the door. I invited them in and tried to make them feel comfortable. Then I rushed to the kitchen, filled the water glasses, dished out food, and seated my guests. After prayer, it suddenly occurred to me that now I was also responsible to keep the conversation flowing. Suddenly I was tired. I had not anticipated this being a part of my job as hostess. My dinner was flawless, but I didn't have time to transition from being a cook to being a conversationalist. I discovered that hospitality included much more than food.

A single woman is a solo hostess. Her success in hospitality hinges upon her ability to be flexible and wear various hats. She is the chief hostess, chef, server, conversationalist, and activities director. Guests will expect her to be in charge. When she appears comfortable in her various roles, her guests will be at ease and enjoy their time. All of this requires preparation!

Know what kind of a person you are with food. Do you love cooking? Then making formal meals may be an outlet for such creativity. Does preparing food intimidate you? By all means, keep it simple. You might consider a potluck of sorts. Or maybe you'll find it easier to throw something on the grill and complete the menu with a salad, hot side dish, and dessert. Working women may not always have time to cook. You can host by buying subs and chips at a local deli or taking your friends to a café.

A woman will enjoy her guests more if she is not racing around at the last minute with food preparations. Stick to a few basic menus and prepare as much ahead of time as possible. Keeping a bag of chicken breasts in your freezer allows for a quick grilled chicken dinner when you add a box of fettuccine pasta or rice pilaf. A batch of chocolate chip cookie dough in the fridge provides an easy treat for expected or unexpected guests. Serve these warm with a scoop of vanilla ice cream and drizzle some hot fudge syrup on top with a dollop of whipped cream.

Although food is an important aspect of hospitality, atmosphere is yet another thing to consider. When you invite guests, prepare a homey atmosphere with things your guests will see, feel, and experience. Ask God to bless the time and fill your home with light and peace. What could be used as an attractive or unusual centerpiece for your table? Display magazines and books your guests can read while you take care of last-minute business in the kitchen. Have soft music playing as your company arrives. Let your guests assist you in setting food on the table. They will feel honored to help in this way.

> The atmosphere you provide is much more important than the type of refreshment you serve, the games you plan, or the decorations you use. Try to have comfortable seating with chairs that face

*each other in an informal circle so guests can see
and hear each other. If you have tables or trays,
place them within easy reach so your guests have
a place to set their drinks while they're visiting.*[5]

Not always do things turn out as we anticipate. One Sunday I invited to lunch a good friend who had recently returned from serving at a mission in Poland. Arriving home after church, I discovered to my dismay that I had overcooked the pasta. I did what another friend, Marie, had exemplified to me in numerous meals at her home. I didn't apologize profusely. I simply stated what happened, and we sat down and ate the mushy pasta with our Alfredo sauce. It did not spoil our afternoon. The focus was not on the pasta, but celebrating the gift of our time together.

Hospitality provides a platform that formal settings do not for blessing and bonding with friends. When you begin sharing from your home food, fun, and fellowship, you offer your guests a taste of God's goodness and love.

Your home is designed by God as a place in which to rest, restore, and reach out. Enjoy the life and love He provides for you there! Let Him be the center of your home, and learn to maximize the resources He has generously given you. Invite others to join you in celebrating His gifts. You will soon discover that He has given your heart a home and a place to belong.

chapter twelve

WEARING THE GLASS SLIPPERS

The long-awaited day finally arrived for the June bride. As lovely wedding music filled the sanctuary, a holy and expectant hush rested upon the seated guests. Eagerly, the attendees turned their heads to watch the beautiful bridesmaids in colorful, shimmering dresses walk down the aisle. Then the moment came for the bride to make her queenly entry. Her simple yet elegant white dress accentuated the glow of her radiant face and sparkling eyes. When she caught the first glimpse of her forty-year-old bridegroom, her mouth broke into wreaths of smiles. This was her day to have and to hold the man she loved.

The thirty-four-year-old bride, my friend Barb, began speaking her vows of commitment to a man worthy of her heart and her love. Neither she nor her bridegroom had ever made these vows before. "I, Barbara, take you, Jason, to be my wedded husband, to have and to hold from this day forward..." The spoken vows of the bride and groom resonated with emotion and deep commitment. Silence breathed as the sacred moment passed, and the postlude began. People stirred in the pews and transitioned into a celebratory mood.

Barb and Jason's wedding day might seem a fairytale of sorts. Their courtship had come to a screeching halt at one point in their lives, and they had gone their separate ways. Each wondered if marriage would ever be a reality for them. Would the broken pieces emerge in oneness for God's purpose and glory? They both clung to the hope that God would direct their paths, although their dreams seemed permanently shattered. Oh, glorious day, when the prince found his Cinderella, and Barb alone could wear the glass slipper Jason held in his hand!

CINDERELLA

Of all the fairytales and folk stories I heard as a child, *Cinderella* always held the most fascination for me. The story depicts deplorable tragedy that ultimately leads to powerful resolution when all that was wrong is finally made right. We are drawn to such stories because of their redemptive themes. In our fallen world, we long for the righting of all things. God's story always promises redemption and resolution. He brings justice to the evil and shows kindness and mercy to the good.

The story of Cinderella begins with the tragic circumstances of misfortune and poverty. Her mother dies and her father re-marries. As the odd stepchild, Cinderella becomes an unwanted intruder. She is expected to obey every whim of her stepsisters and stepmother. It appears that Cinderella will never rise from the despicable fate that binds her to menial servitude.

Her father is an uninvolved character in the story, whose absence leaves Cinderella weak and defenseless. She aches for deliverance. The story's setting prepares the reader to anticipate resolution for her. Its development pulls the reader to feel revulsion toward the evil she encounters and to cheer the good fortune that comes to her at last.

This fairy tale has, of course, the basic literary components of setting, characters, plot, and final resolution. Yet its impact does not stand on these merits, but on the tale's underlying themes. The powerful medium of story connects with our hearts, forming a bridge that links the themes of its characters' lives to the themes of our own lives. The compelling theme of *Cinderella* is that good will triumph over evil. We love the story because it stirs hope within our hearts.

PART OF THE STORY

After everyone in the house departed for the palace ball, Cinder Wench (as she was called by her stepsisters) crept to a cold, dark corner and wept. All day she had watched and assisted her stepsisters as they primped and preened for the evening social whirl. While the stepsisters twittered and giggled, Cinderella could scarcely imagine the delight of wearing a swirling gown and mingling with others in the beauty of the palace.

That evening she sat alone—a forlorn and bedraggled girl with patches on her dress and soot on her nose. Tears trickled silently down her cheeks. She shivered in the damp room and watched a little mouse nibbling on a morsel. How she longed for the beauty and goodness that could transport her from the dungeon of gloom to the palace of lights!

Suddenly Cinderella blinked. In a glow of light, her fairy godmother appeared before her, offering kindness and hope.

With a wave of her wand, she transformed Cinderella into an elegant young lady with an exquisite gown and all the accessories, including a dainty pair of glass slippers. She was destined for far more than she could ever imagine!

The wand also provided a carriage complete with white horses and a coachman. As Cinderella stepped into the carriage, her godmother presented one stipulation—she must be home by midnight. That magical hour would cause all her finery to vanish.

Every head turned as Cinderella walked into the palace that evening, and the prince found himself drawn to her side. She was the envy of everyone present, and not even her stepsisters recognized the transformation.

The evening hours passed quickly. Before Cinderella knew it, midnight had come. She hurriedly left the palace and the prince at the stroke of midnight. In her haste, she left behind one glass slipper as she all but flew down the palace steps.

This is almost the end of the story, but not quite. The plot thickens. Darkness and despair reached out their fingers to consume her once again, but this time she refused to succumb to their voices. She held to one hope. Perhaps, just perhaps, the prince would remember her and come in search of her. In her hasty flight, one swift backward glance told her the prince had picked up the glass slipper. Cinderella clung not only to the memory, but also to the slipper's mate, which she treasured in her pocket.

Days later, the royal carriage stopped abruptly at Cinderella and her stepsisters' home. Her heart quickened. Entering the house, the prince made known his intentions. He wanted to marry the woman who could wear the glass slipper left on the stairway of the palace. The stepsisters smiled knowingly at each other. Surely theirs would be the good fortune. But alas, neither stepsister could wear the dainty shoe.

"I would like to try on the slipper," Cinderella said softly.

The young prince caught sight of Cinderella and smiled. Determined to leave no stone unturned, he insisted that she try on the glass slipper, all the while ignoring the angry mutters and withering glances of the stepsisters. With a flushed face, Cinderella walked gracefully to the chair proffered her. She held out her foot. The glass slipper fit. She had waited, and her prince had come.

THE PRINCE OF PEACE COMES

Why do we sigh with delight and feel a twinge of desire after we read such a fairy tale? Like Cinderella, every woman experiences disappointment and failure. We groan in our earthly rags of mortality. We mourn the mistakes and stains of our souls.

However, the gospel brings us hope in our plight. The good news does not stake its hope on a figment of imagination—a make-believe fairy godmother—but on the coming of Jesus Christ. He came as the Prince of Peace, through a young virgin over two thousand years ago. Mary was quietly going about her business when she had an encounter with God that forever changed her destiny and ours.

Mary's heritage boasted a lineage of kings. But Mary did not reside in a palace as the daughter of a royal ruler, with a stash of purple and fine linen at her disposal. Mary was a single woman betrothed to a carpenter. She and Joseph were young people of meager means, living ordinary lives. They resided in the obscure village of Nazareth during a difficult historical period when the Roman Empire controlled their beloved country, Israel.

The Jewish people had heard very little from God in the past four hundred years. Now God was ready to make His appearance! His coming was announced to Mary by the angel Gabriel. Gabriel didn't wave a magic wand and change all of Mary's disappointing circumstances in that moment. Rather, he spoke three blessings upon Mary that forever changed her perspective and destiny. He promised her the blessings of grace, presence, and provision.

Gabriel spoke the first blessing with these words, "'Rejoice, highly favored one'" (Luke 1:28). *Highly favored* comes from the Greek root word *charis*, which is often translated *grace.*[1] Thus the first blessing came as a gift of grace to Mary. Though we often think of grace as "favor shown to one who is undeserving," *charis* means far more than that. The word carries connotations of pleasure, delight, sweetness, charm, and loveliness. God loved Mary as a chosen daughter—a "highly favored one" of His own. And His grace enabled her, surrounding and protecting her at every turn in this journey. "Mary was to bear Jesus Christ, the whole treasure of God's grace, in her womb."[2]

The second blessing imparted upon Mary involved presence. Gabriel said, "'The Lord is with you'" (Luke 1:28). The little preposition *with* carries much weight in the Greek rendering. It "strictly implies motion towards the middle or into the midst of anything...so as to follow and be with a person."[3] She would not be alone as she carried the Prince of Peace in her womb. She need not succumb to panic or fear. The very presence of God would envelop her and protect her.

Finally, Mary heard the third blessing spoken to her by

Gabriel—a blessing of provision. "'Blessed are you among women!'" (Luke 1:28). Mary would experience sorrow and pain as a woman. However, these could never annul God's blessings. People can bless each other with words, but "when the subject is God, His speaking is His action...He acts for our good as He sees what we need most and not what we desire."[4] God's blessings on Mary's life did not mean that all of her desires would culminate in perfection. However, His blessing was upon her, and He would act in her best interest and for her good. That is what always happens when God blesses His people!

The Prince of Peace comes to us with the same three blessings God brought to Mary. The gift of grace comes to women who are single. Just as grace enabled Mary to carry the Son of God in her womb, so His enabling grace makes it possible to carry the gift of singleness in our season. We need God's enabling grace every day to bear our gift of virginity with submission and virtue.

You may wonder how this will ever be possible in the face of your desire for marriage and family. You are not alone with such questions. Mary had a question too: "How shall this be, seeing I know not a man?" (Luke 1:34 KJV). The answer for you is the same as it was for Mary, and comes in her second blessing of the promised "'Immanuel...God is with us'" (Matthew 1:23). We are not alone in our singlehood, for His very presence dwells within us. He not only affirms us as His highly favored daughters, but His presence envelops and protects us.

The third blessing Mary received also comes to all single women who turn their faces toward the Father. His blessing of provision works in accordance with His will and purposes (Philippians 2:13). He always acts for our good and in the interest of our needs, but not necessarily according to our desires. In this we can trust Him. Listen for the Prince of Peace, for He comes with grace, presence, and provision! In these blessings, He calls you to worship Him as Mary worshiped the Prince of Peace because of her gifts.

THE PRINCE OF PEACE IS WORSHIPED

A young woman moved into the most shadowy corner of the large room. She stood silent, partially hidden by a thick curtain. Small oil lamps illuminated the walls, casting dancing shadows that heightened the room's activity. A long, low table stretched across the center of the room. Ranged around it, thirteen reclining men finished their meal. The woman paused, fingering the smooth curves of the jar hidden under the folds of her soft garment.

Her eyes rested upon the Guest of Honor. He looked fatigued, but His weathered face broke into a grin as the other men guffawed at Peter's story. A bearded servant carrying a flask of wine walked past her. She would wait a few more minutes until the Guest had His beverage, and then she would bring Him her gift.

Suddenly the Guest noticed her. His eyes spoke kindness and mercy. Oblivious to the boisterous voices and raucous laughter, she caught the eyes that compelled her to walk straight toward Him. Eagerly she came to His side to offer her gift of love.

Quietly she knelt before Him. Deftly she pulled the jar from beneath the folds of her robe and lightly tapped it against the stone floor. The jar's neck broke, and she poured the expensive ointment, nard, onto Jesus' feet. Gently she rubbed the weary, calloused feet that had walked many miles to reach Bethany.

Silent tears mingled with the ointment. Intent on this Man, she was oblivious to the hush that fell over the others as the scent permeated the room.

"Scandalous!" she heard someone cry out scornfully. Looking up, Mary saw the shocked faces of twelve men and twelve pairs of accusing eyes.

"A year's wages poured out on two feet. I say it should have been sold and the money given to the poor!" another man added angrily.

Confused and hurt, Mary looked at Jesus. He nodded lovingly. "Do what you must, Mary," He whispered to her. Then He turned to speak to the outraged men.

Quietly sobbing now, Mary bent low, letting her veil slide to her lap. Taking her long, loose hair she began wiping Jesus' feet and whispering her adoration. She knew He had received her acts of worship and love.

Mary's unrestrained worship was not intended to be offensive. Her one purpose and aim was to express total devotion to her Prince of Peace. I am reminded of a statement I heard from Pastor John Coblentz. He said Mary gave the best she had when she offered the nard, and she gave the best of who she was when she wiped Jesus' feet with her hair. I believe that in her worship she gave the most costly gifts she had in her possession, the precious nard and her beautiful tresses.

She offered not symbolic expressions of love, but the deepest and most tangible realities of her devotion. She poured out nard with the heart of a servant and humbly wiped His feet with the glory of her femininity. The Prince of Peace condemns no woman worshiping Him with such lavish devotion. He delights in receiving our expressions of worship when we come to Him in the realization of our need and His worthiness. In our worship we open our hearts to meet Him in the most surprising moments, as did a third Mary, Mary Magdalene.

THE PRINCE OF PEACE RULES

Mary Magdalene's heart lurched. Something seemed strange. Peering through the pale dawn, she and her friends suddenly realized that the great stone had been rolled away from the sepulcher. Hesitating, they stared at each other with consternation and surprise. Just moments before, they had been discussing the dilemma of the stone-sealed tomb. Now the giant obstacle had been totally removed. Salome whispered, "Shall we go and see if Jesus is still there?"

Mary Magdalene nodded. The brisk morning breeze tugged at her veil. Reaching up, she wrapped it more snugly about her head and quickened her pace toward the dark cave. With trepidation, her friends followed more slowly. Then Mary Magdalene froze. Jesus' body was gone! She whirled around and motioned the others to hurry. "S-s-someone s-stole Him," she stammered.

Shocked and paralyzed, the small group of women huddled together. Suddenly two men in shining garments appeared before their eyes. "Why do you seek the living among the dead?" they asked.

Trembling with fear and the first dawn of joy, the women fell to their faces. The angels reminded them of what Jesus had prophesied concerning His crucifixion and resurrection. "Now go," they instructed. "Tell the disciples what you have seen."

Running back to the city, the women found Jesus' friends and breathlessly told of their morning adventure.

When Peter and John ran to see the sepulcher for themselves, Mary followed. But this time the tomb was empty except for the folded napkin and linen grave clothes. No angel visitants confirmed to the disciples the story of resurrection. Uncertain what to do, the two men finally returned to their homes. Mary Magdalene, however, stayed near the sepulcher, weeping. If Jesus was alive, where was He? The events of the past few days seemed wildly out of control. Everything seemed so confusing, with grief and joy, hope and despair, mixed all together.

Mary Magdalene brought her love and tears to the tomb that Easter morning. Its death-like atmosphere reeked of evil. A broken, bleeding Man had been placed there, and now even His body was gone, her last link to Him broken. In her distress, the angels' promises brought her little comfort. She just could not grasp the implications of all that was happening.

Through her tears she caught sight of movement in the tomb. Looking inside again, she saw two angels. "Why are you weeping?" they asked.

Distraught, she dabbed at her eyes with her veil. "Someone came and took away my Lord, and I don't know where they have laid Him," she moaned.

Someone came up behind Mary. "Woman," He asked, "why are you weeping? Whom are you seeking?"

Sobbing she implored Him, "Sir, if you have taken His body away, just tell me where you put Him! I will take Him away."

Then Jesus said one word. "Mary!"

Mary Magdalene whirled about to face Him. "Master!" she

replied incredulously.

At last, joy swept away all confusion and doubt. With absolute authority Jesus spoke, "I ascend unto my Father, and your Father, and to my God, and your God."

When Jesus showed up, Mary Magdalene seemed more thrilled than shocked. Why shouldn't she be? All that had been wrong was made right. She became certain of His sovereignty— of His ability to triumph over every situation, causing even the worst evil to accomplish His purposes. In essence, Jesus told her that His ascension completed the work of salvation. He would sit at the Father's right hand (Ephesians 1:20) and live forever to make intercession for us (Hebrews 7:25).

He, the Prince of Peace, rules forever and ever; His reign knows no end (Revelation 11:15). In His reign "'Every valley shall be exalted and every mountain and hill brought low; the crooked places shall be made straight and the rough places smooth; the glory of the LORD shall be revealed, and all flesh shall see it together; for the mouth of the LORD has spoken'" (Isaiah 40:4-5). What hope this brings to us as single women! Our Prince of Peace is in control of this world, and in control of our lives. He rules with absolute authority and power.

We have looked at three women called Mary. Each of them received a precious gift from the Prince of Peace. Mary, the mother of Jesus, received the gift of Him within herself. Mary of Bethany received the gift of His kindness and mercy. Mary Magdalene received the gift of His sovereignty—His breathtaking, trustworthy arrangement of every event of her life. These gifts came at a price. His blood had to be shed so the women might live in relationship with Him, forever. They understood this, and in return they gave their hearts unreservedly to Him.

Frederick Buechner, a theologian and author, once wrote that "the gospel is part tragedy, part comedy, and part fairy tale. The *tragedy* is that we have estranged ourselves from God, making us unlovable. The comedy is that, even so, he invited us to the ball. The fairy tale is that not only are we invited to the ball, but we will be transformed so that we will be fit for the ball."[5] The fact is that our transformation is NO fairy tale, but a Truth grounded in the person of Jesus Christ.

TO HAVE AND TO HOLD

As unmarried daughters of God, we must recognize that not all will be perfect in this fallen world. We are not home yet. Our hearts still long at times for a prince with a glass slipper. We yearn for completion and connection. That is why we wipe tears when the bride and groom seal their vows with the promise "to have and to hold, from this day forward..." To have and to hold—we can only shake our heads at the mystery of such oneness. Yet even in the best of earthly marriages, the "having and holding" falters.

Who is there, then, to love us unreservedly, exclusively, and unendingly? Who is there to hold us in an eternal embrace—to protect us, shelter us, and fight for us? You do have a Prince. I have a Prince. The Prince of Peace has come to us, and *will* come for us. When He comes, all that is wrong with the world will be made right. It is this hope that gives us the ability to live in a fallen world, a world that is in opposition to everything that points toward God. And that is not all. There is more to the story. Read on!

Our Prince of Peace is the Bridegroom. Imagine! Doesn't

that just about leave you breathless? Our union with Him will be wildly superior to any earthly marriage or any glass slipper a human prince could offer. Single people will not miss out on this marriage! There is a marriage supper of the Lamb pending, and we are called to participate as Jesus' chosen bride. This is redeeming love!

Despite the sacredness of marital intimacy on earth, it is only a partial picture of what God intends in the consummation of all things for Jesus Christ and His bride, the church. What is now withheld from single people will not be withheld in the new heaven and new earth. What now remains a mystery to singles will then be revealed in their redeemed bodies. We are invited to experience the ultimate completion and connection, the reality that the deepest of earthly unions was only foreshadowing. Our ecstasy will know no limits when we bring our gifts of virginity and fidelity to the marriage supper of the Lamb.

Eugene Peterson's paraphrase of II Corinthians 4:16-18 in *The Message* aptly captures the focus of an eternal perspective. I have drawn encouragement from these words many times.

> *So we're not giving up. How could we!*
> *Even though on the outside it often looks*
> *like things are falling apart on us,*
> *on the inside, where God is making new life,*
> *not a day goes by without his unfolding grace.*
> *These hard times are small potatoes*
> *compared to the coming good times,*
> *the lavish celebration prepared for us.*
> *There's far more here than meets the eye.*

The things we see now are here today, gone tomorrow.

But the things we can't see now will last forever.

This is why we do not lose heart if the earthly glass slipper doesn't show up within our time frame. God will not forget us. God is with us. And God will come. We have this promise, and we hold to this promise (See Hebrews 10:37).

God often comes when we least expect Him. When He shows up, we will know it is He! Many times I am reminded of that powerful truth when I glance at my bone-colored creamer from Aunt Emma. The creamer no longer sits alone in my house. Hundreds of miles from my home, I stumbled across its partner years later in a most surprising way. The paired sugar and creamer set in my kitchen is a constant reminder that God does come. If God can complete a sugar and creamer set, how much more will He complete our lives as single women with His coming!

I remain a single woman today. My season of singleness has been longer than I could ever have envisioned in my twenties. But in my singleness, the Prince of Peace has come to me. I **have** His presence, and I **hold** to His promises. He whispers His love, His faithfulness, His mercy. I have come to trust His embrace. In His arms I rest, and I am fully satisfied.

* * * * * * *

The LORD your God in your midst,
The Mighty One, will save;
He will rejoice over you with gladness,
He will quiet you with His love,
He will rejoice over you with singing.

ZEPHANIAH 3.17

ENDNOTES

CHAPTER ONE

1. James Strong, *Strong's Exhaustive Concordance of the Bible: The Greek Dictionary of the New Testament* (New York: Abingdon Press, 1970), 36.

CHAPTER TWO

1. Spiros Zodhiates, *The Complete Word Study Old Testament* (Iowa Falls: World Bible Publishers, 1988), 1648.
2. Nancy Groom, *Heart to Heart about Men: Words of Encouragement for Women of Integrity* (Colorado Springs: NavPress, 1995), 21.
3. Spiros Zodhiates, *The Complete Word Study Old Testament*, 2303.
4. Walter Wangerin, Jr., *As for Me and My House*, 60.

CHAPTER THREE

1. Carolyn McCulley, *Did I Kiss Marriage Goodbye?* (Wheaton, IL: Crossway Books, 2004), 61.
2. James Strong, *Strong's Exhaustive Concordance of the Bible: The Greek Dictionary of the New Testament*, 29.
3. *Webster's New World College Dictionary* (New York: Macmillan, 1997), 447.
4. *Webster's New World College Dictionary*, 16.
5. *Webster's New World College Dictionary*, 283.
6. Spiros Zodhiates, *The Complete Word Study Old Testament*, 2304.
7. Larry Crabb, *The Silence of Adam* (Grand Rapids, MI: Zondervan, 1995), 93.
8. Nancy Groom, *Heart to Heart about Men: Words of Encouragement for Women of Integrity*, 17.
9. Anita Yoder, *Life is for Living: not for waiting around* (Printed in USA, 2008), 63.

CHAPTER FOUR

1. Marilyn McGinnis, *Single* (Old Tappan, NJ: Spire Books, 1974), 18.
2. Nancy Groom, *Heart to Heart about Men: Words of Encouragement for Women of Integrity*, 25.
3. John Coblentz, *Christian Family Living* (Harrisonburg, VA: Christian Light Publications, 1997), 110.
4. Dan B. Allender, *The Healing Path* (Colorado Springs: Waterbrook Press, 1999), 205-206.
5. Dan B. Allender, *The Healing Path*, 189.

CHAPTER FIVE

1. Spiros Zodhiates, *The Hebrew-Greek Study Bible* (Iowa Falls: World Bible Publishers, 1988), 76.
2. Nancy Groom, *Heart to Heart about Men: Words of Encouragement for Women of Integrity*, 156.
3. Larry Crabb, *Inside Out* (Colorado Springs: NavPress, 1990), 149.

CHAPTER SIX

1. Bruce Yoder and Imo Jeanne Yoder, *Single Voices* (Scottdale, PA: Herald Press, 1982), 64.
2. *Webster's New World College Dictionary*, 1230.
3. Kathleen Kingsbury, "Pregnancy Boom at Gloucester High School." Time Magazine. 18 June 2008. <www.time.com/time/magazine/article/0,9171,1816486,00.html>
4. Nancy Groom, *Heart to Heart about Men: Words of Encouragement for Women of Integrity*, 115.
5. Bruce Yoder and Imo Jeanne Yoder, *Single Voices*, 65.
6. Paula Rinehart, *Strong Women, Soft Hearts* (Nashville, TN: Thomas Nelson, 2001), 104-105.
7. Shannon Ethridge, *Every Woman's Battle* (Colorado Springs: WaterBrook Press, 2003), 23.
8. Paula Rinehart, *Strong Women, Soft Hearts*, 25.
9. Evelyn King Mumaw, *Woman Alone* (Scottdale, PA: Herald Press, 1970), 82-83.
10. Paula Rinehart, *Sex and the Soul of a Woman* (Grand Rapids, MI: Zondervan, 2004), 95.
11. Toni Grant, *Being a Woman* (New York: Avon Books, 1989), 104.

CHAPTER SEVEN

1. Dan Allender, *Cry of the Soul* (Colorado Springs: NavPress, 1994), 24.
2. Fred H. Wight, *Manners and Customs of Bible Lands* (Chicago: Moody Press, 1983), 128.
3. Fred H. Wight, *Manners and Customs of Bible Lands*, 108.
4. Elizabeth Elliot, *The Path of Loneliness* (Nashville: Thomas Nelson, 1988), 26.
5. Fred H. Wight, *Manners and Customs of Bible Lands*, 129.
6. Mike Mason, *The Mystery of Marriage* (Sisters, OR: Multnomah Books, 1985), 174.
7. *Webster's New World College Dictionary*, 1232.
8. Dan Allender, *Cry of the Soul*, 199.
9. Dan Allender, *Cry of the Soul*, 202.
10. Thomas à Kempis, *The Imitation of Christ* in an anthology entitled *The Consolation of Philosophy* (New York: Random House, 1943), 139.

CHAPTER EIGHT

1. Carolyn McCulley, *Did I Kiss Marriage Goodbye?*, 152.
2. Carolyn McCulley, *Did I Kiss Marriage Goodbye?*, 150.
3. Elizabeth Elliot, *The Path of Loneliness*, 117.
4. Carolyn McCulley, *Did I Kiss Marriage Goodbye?*, 153.
5. Eugenia Price, *God Speaks to Women Today* (Grand Rapids, MI: Zondervan, 1964), 186.
6. Evelyn King Mumaw, *Woman Alone*, 62-63.
7. Hannah Hurnard, *Hinds' Feet on High Places* (Wheaton, IL: Living Books Tyndale House, 1975), 248.
8. Philip Yancey, *Disappointment with God* (New York: Harper, 1988), 217-218.
9. Philip Yancey, *Disappointment with God*, 55.

CHAPTER NINE

1. *Webster's New World College Dictionary*, 1132.
2. *Webster's New World College Dictionary*, 540.
3. As reported in Washington Post, "Enough Talk, Already." Aug 21, 2007, Laura Sessions Stepp.
4. Dee Brestin, *The Friendships of Women* (Colorado Springs: David C. Cook, 2008), 17.

CHAPTER TEN

1. *Webster's New World College Dictionary*, 1500.
2. Mark Twain, *Tom Sawyer* (New York: Harper, 1920), 71.
3. Paula Rinehart, *Sex and the Soul of a Woman*, 97.
4. Paula Rinehart, *Sex and the Soul of a Woman*, 97.
5. Shannon Ethridge, *Every Woman's Battle*, 94.
6. Nancy Groom, *Heart to Heart about Men: Words of Encouragement for Women of Integrity*, 17.
7. Leslie Ludy, *Authentic Beauty: The Shaping of a Set-Apart Young Woman*, (Colorado Springs: Multnomah Books, 2007), 170.

CHAPTER ELEVEN

1. Carolyn McCulley, *Did I Kiss Marriage Goodbye?*, 155-156.
2. Spiros Zodhiates, *The Complete Word Study Old Testament*, 2305.
3. Edith Schaeffer, *What Is a Family?* (Old Tappan, NJ: Fleming H. Revell, 1975), 220.
4. Rachael Crabb, *The Personal Touch: Encouraging Others Through Hospitality* (Colorado Springs, NavPress, 1990), 71.
5. Rachael Crabb, *The Personal Touch: Encouraging Others Through Hospitality*, 30.

CHAPTER TWELVE

1. Spiros Zodhiates, *The Complete Word Study New Testament* (Chattanooga, TN: AMG Publishers, 1991), 967.
2. Spiros Zodhiates, *The Complete Word Study New Testament*, 967.
3. Spiros Zodhiates, *The Complete Word Study New Testament*, 930.
4. Spiros Zodhiates, *The Complete Word Study New Testament*, 917.
5. Ken Gire, *The Divine Embrace* (Wheaton, IL: Tyndale House, 2003), 208-209.

Sharon Yoder holds both a B.S. and an M.A. degree in elementary education with a teaching career of about thirty years. Much of her classroom experience has included teaching upper elementary grades which she finds invigorating and rewarding. Fifth and sixth grade students' energy and eagerness to learn new concepts make teaching a joy.

Sharon has also been a part-time instructor at Faith Builders Educational Programs—a two-year biblical training institute in the Anabaptist heritage that prepares teachers for conservative Mennonite schools. Additionally, this institution offers a biblical worldview program. This has given Sharon speaking, mentoring, and teaching opportunities to a variety of single and married women.

Preparing food in her kitchen and entertaining guests help keep Sharon's life in balance. She treasures time spent with her family and friends. When a quiet evening finds her, she might curl up with a good book or take a walk in the wilderness areas near her home.

SHARON'S BLOG
www.tohaveandtoholdbook.com

Are you looking for a pause in life's journey? A place to set aside the ordinary demands of today and restore your hope for tomorrow?

Visit Sharon's blog for a bit of encouragement and learn to know the author of *To Have and To Hold* more fully. This is also a place to respond to the book or to hear what others are saying.

Bring a cup of tea and welcome!